LEAD

T0045627

LEAD

50 Models for Success
in Work & Life

John D H Greenway
Andy Blacknell
Andy Coombe

This edition first published 2018

© 2018 Saltmine Ventures Ltd., Blacknell Ventures Ltd., Kairos Consultancy Ltd.

Registered office

John Wiley & Sons Ltd., The Atrium, Southern Gate, Chichester, West Sussex, PO19 8SQ, United Kingdom

For details of our global editorial offices, for customer services and for information about how to apply for permission to reuse the copyright material in this book please see our website at www.wiley.com.

John D H Greenway, Andy Blacknell, and Andy Coombe have asserted their rights under the Copyright, Designs and Patents Act 1988 to be identified as the authors of this work. Illustrations by Bryan Mathers, Visual Thinkery.

All rights reserved. No part of this publication may be reproduced, stored in a retrieval system, or transmitted in any form or by any means, electronic, mechanical, photocopying, recording, or otherwise, without the prior permission of the copyright owner.

Wiley publishes in a variety of print and electronic formats and by print-on-demand. Some material included with standard print versions of this book may not be included in e-books or in print-on-demand. If this book refers to media such as a CD or DVD that is not included in the version you purchased, you may download this material at http://booksupport.wiley.com. For more information about Wiley products, visit www.wiley.com.

Designations used by companies to distinguish their products are often claimed as trademarks. All brand names and product names used in this book are trade names, service marks, trademarks, or registered trademarks of their respective owners. The publisher is not associated with any product or vendor mentioned in this book.

Limit of Liability/Disclaimer of Warranty: While the publisher and authors have used their best efforts in preparing this book, they make no representations or warranties with respect to the accuracy or completeness of the contents of this book and specifically disclaim any implied warranties of merchantability or fitness for a particular purpose. It is sold on the understanding that the publisher is not engaged in rendering professional services and neither the publisher nor the authors shall be liable for damages arising herefrom. If professional advice or other expert assistance is required, the services of a competent professional should be sought.

Library of Congress Cataloging-in-Publication Data is available

A catalogue record for this book is available from the British Library.

ISBN 978-0-857-08791-1 (pbk) ISBN 978-0-857-08796-6 (ebk)
ISBN 978-0-857-08795-9 (ebk)

Cover Design: Wiley

Set in 10.5/13 Avenir LT Std by Aptara Inc., New Delhi, India

Printed in Great Britain by TJ International Ltd., Padstow, Cornwall, UK

10 9 8 7 6 5 4 3 2 1

Contents

Dashboard

LEAD will equip you to lead and succeed in work and life.

This Dashboard will guide you through the book:

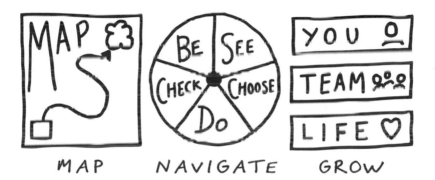

LEAD   NAVIGATE   GROW

LEAD will equip you with enduring principles, inspiring stories and practical tools to:

- **Map** the journeys that you want to make in work and life
- **Navigate** you and your team through life's twists and turns to success
- **Grow** your personal capacity and develop the potential of others

Let's get going.

PART ONE

Map

Map out your future, but do it in pencil.
Jon Bon Jovi

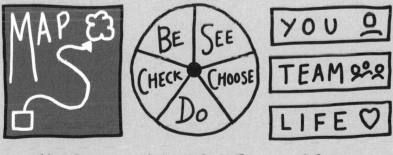

MAP   NAVIGATE   GROW

Life is not a straight line

No one is so brave that he is not disturbed by something unexpected.

Julius Caesar

Andrew's Story

'Hey Andrew', said the voice on the phone, 'It's your father. You need to come home. We're closing the business.'

Andrew O'Shaughnessy's world was rocked to the core. Away studying business strategy, his life had been planned for the day when he would take over the family woollen mill in Dripsey, a small village in rural Ireland. His father, his grandfather and his great grandfather had laid the pathway for him. They were proud to supply the best outlets in London, New York, Paris and Milan. And now it was all falling apart around his ears.

Andrew jumped on the first plane home and begged for one last chance to save the mill. He met with each of the 88 workers and set out the bare facts. Like him, they and their forebears had worked in the mill for generations.

Someone must have an idea. There must be some way to save the business and all their jobs. But no.

Andrew held his head in his hands. An old hand approached him. 'We've never been asked for our ideas before. We didn't think it was our place. We've done what you and your family have asked us to do. We're used to you having the answers, not us.'

No-one had expected this.

So 88 good people lost their jobs, 88 families their livelihoods. Many of them would never work again. They had no other skills, no other options. This was their life. It was too late to change.

Andrew swore he would never again put himself in the position of being responsible for the loss of so many livelihoods. So he moved to London and, for the best part of a decade, drifted from one freelance role to another.

Convinced finally that it must be possible to be successful and still treat people well, the prodigal returned to his Irish home ready to start a new business. His small start-up tech business was situated in a business park where Amazon, Apple and Dell EMC were among his neighbours.

Fast-forward another decade, and once again Andrew held his head in his hands.

He had employed Sinead for a year, and thought he knew her well. She had just come up with a brilliant solution that would save the business. But why had she waited so long to offer her thoughts?

'I didn't think it was my place', she explained.

'What? It's *always* your place to bring forward the solutions', he said despairingly.

It was a bombshell. Andrew couldn't believe that 20 years after he'd closed down his family business in Ireland, history seemed destined to repeat itself.

He wanted everyone to behave like they owned the business. He had strong values, honed in the hard knocks of the family mill. He spoke about them endlessly – didn't he? – so how could she not have known?

Despite his best efforts, had he recreated the disastrous 'them and us', paternalistic culture of the family woollen mill? But for Sinead's intervention, the company might have gone bust. He had to go back to the drawing board and think again.

Another ten years on, and Andrew O'Shaughnessy now leads *Poppulo*, with a crystal clear vision – 'to make companies great by releasing the power of their people'.

The journey has had many twists and turns. From email marketing to internal staff communications, *Poppulo* now aims to lead the field in staff engagement across America and Europe. They serve leading global companies – Unilever, Barclays, Lloyds, Coca-Cola, Nike, Adidas, Danone, Nestlé and countless others. Their numbers keep growing.

But throughout these changes, Andrew's values have not migrated an inch, only strengthened. From the closure of the woollen mill, to the encounter with Sinead, to serving some of the largest organisations on the planet, he has always said: 'It's about the people'.

He is emphatic: 'Make the people a real part of your business by unleashing their individual strengths. It's not an easy ride, but it will dramatically increase your chances of success.'

Zigzag Leadership

Consider Andrew's story. Look at your *own* story. Look where you are, and trace the path you took getting here. Your job, your home, your family. Has your life to this point been a straight line? Could you have predicted where you are now 20 years ago? Or ten? Or even one year ago?

Life is not a straight line.

LEADERS' MAP STORYBOARD

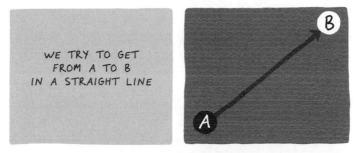

WE TRY TO GET
FROM A TO B
IN A STRAIGHT LINE

...BUT LIFE IS UNPREDICTABLE & CIRCUMSTANCES CHANGE

WINDS BLOW...
WAVES RISE...
CURRENTS PULL...
OBSTACLES BLOCK &
OPPORTUNITIES ARISE

OUR JOURNEY IS MORE LIKE SAILING
THAN DRIVING ALONG A STRAIGHT ROAD

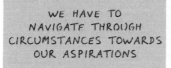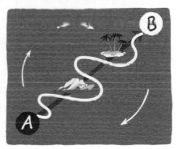

WE HAVE TO
NAVIGATE THROUGH
CIRCUMSTANCES TOWARDS
OUR ASPIRATIONS

*Previous journeys in search of treasure have taught me
that a zigzag strategy is the best way to get ahead.*
Tahir Shah

We live in a highly changing and dynamic world. Our twenty-first century environment is volatile, uncertain, complex and ambiguous. So is your journey – in whatever aspect of your life you want to focus on.

Your journey is more like sailing uncharted waters than driving along a straight road. It's more akin to stormy seas than tree-lined avenues. You are going where no-one has gone before.

At sea there are no signposts to tell you to turn right or left. You have to use your judgement to zig or zag, otherwise you can blissfully go way off course while you think you are sailing well.

That's the art of leading.

Leadership is taking people with you on a journey of common purpose and direction.

The journey won't be easy. Winds blow, waves rise and currents pull. Unseen obstacles block your way and unexpected opportunities present themselves. To get to where you have been before is relatively easy. You just need a plan. But to get to where no-one has been before, you first need to map the territory; *then* you can plan your course.

But static plans and strategies can't take account of shifting seas and changing weather. In the words of President Dwight D. Eisenhower, 'Plans are nothing; planning is everything.'

As the architect of the D-Day landings, he knew a thing or two about plans and planning. Plans are static, planning is active. The plan is useful for as long as nothing changes. Planning is critical all the time.

Mapping is more than just creating a plan or having a strategy. It is a dynamic, ongoing activity that responds to the changing environment and plots the evolving journey.

Focus 1

Map Your Journey

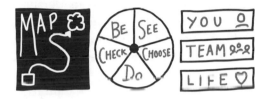

Twenty years from now you will be more disappointed by the things you didn't do than by the things you did do, so throw off the bowlines, sail away from safe harbour, catch the trade winds in your sails. Explore. Dream. Discover.

Mark Twain

As Andrew navigated from point to point, he always needed to have a clear idea of where he was heading – the purpose and direction of the journey. This is your **vision**.

Andrew would describe his vision as 'making companies great by releasing the power of their people', but that's very different from where he started in the 1990s.

Without this clarity it is easy to follow any wind, or sail towards any calm waters – avoiding trouble, but achieving nothing.

Take a moment and think of your primary leadership role. It might be at work, at home or in a voluntary role. You choose. What is your purpose? What is your big aspiration in the role? What keeps you going? What are you trying to engage others in?

Your vision will be aspirational – inspiring you to strive forward and others to follow you.

So before you go any further, test yourself: just how ambitious is your vision?

Make a note of it:

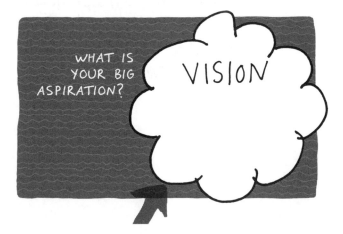

Andrew was crystal clear about how he wanted himself and others to behave as they worked, independently and collaboratively. These are your **values**. They dictate how you will behave, when no-one is watching, even when it is to your short-term detriment. They are your golden rules of life and leadership. They won't change. They describe you, your DNA, to the core.

One of Andrew's primary values is 'Together we're better', so no-one would say, as Sinead had, 'it's not my place'. His bitter experience in the mill means he enshrines the value 'Adapt to succeed'. 'What might have happened with the mill if the workers had had this value?' he reflects wistfully. And a third is 'Be the example', which encapsulates his commitment to producing the best from each person by working as a team. This commitment extends to rallying round any team member who is in trouble. 'We keep everyone in', he says with pride.

Now think who you are. What do you believe? What drives you? What poor behaviours, when seen in others, make you angry? What behaviours are you so stubbornly committed to that you won't compromise, even to your detriment? These are your values. Write them down:

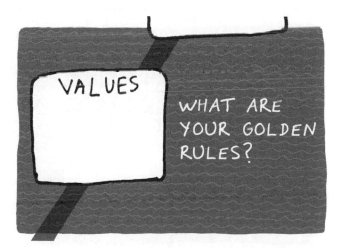

You will give up your vision before you give up your values – but in your heart you are convinced your values will better enable you to reach your vision. Your journey may be a zigzag, but your values will be as straight as an arrow, always linking where you are now to your vision for the future.

Success is measurable. If your vision is big enough, you may never see it all fulfiled. But you will have clear, objective, stretch targets that are nevertheless achievable. They are signposts on the way to your vision, evidence that you are on the right course and succeeding. These are your **goals**.

They will define your actions and conversations as you seek to travel forward. They mark your progress to your ultimate aim. You can point to their success – or failure – with a Yes or a No. There is no ambiguity.

Andrew had an ambitious goal to be the first player in the people engagement field to break through in both the US and European markets. But he began with the medium-term goal of being the market leader in the UK.

Think about what success will look like for you. Identify the top two or at most three concrete goals that in the medium to long term will describe a successful journey towards your vision. Commit to them in writing:

Your *values* will rarely if ever change. Your *vision* may last a lifetime, but it may change slowly over the years. Your *goals* will endure, but change as old goals you have achieved are replaced with new challenging goals to take you further towards your vision. The leader needs to be crystal clear about these, or risk sailing in circles or getting stuck in the doldrums.

But while these change little, your circumstances are changing constantly. So leaders need to be acutely aware of where they are now. How far along are you towards achieving your goals? How are the crew doing? What are the weather conditions like? This is your **current position**.

It's changing moment by moment. If you have no clear vision you will simply react to circumstances. But with clear goals and by being proactive you can read your current situation to see what will help you achieve success and what may hinder you.

Andrew's brutal honesty led to one of his most significant breakthroughs. Having taken 12 months to develop their own software, they emerged to find the market had moved on. He might have just soldiered on. But he recognised quickly that they were dead in the water. This openness to the uncomfortable truth freed him up to look honestly at the risks and opportunities available to him.

If your goals are aligned to your vision, you can simply evaluate your current position against your future goals. Be brutally honest as you describe your current position here:

The external elements that may help are **opportunities**, and those that may hinder are **risks** to your enterprise. But be careful! It takes great wisdom to see the difference. As Winston Churchill said, 'A pessimist sees the difficulty in every opportunity; an optimist sees the opportunity in every difficulty'.

Faced with lagging far behind in one market, Andrew saw an opportunity to lead the market in another. While their product was behind the curve, he started to hear feedback that customers were using his software for totally different purposes – and they loved it! He grasped the opportunity to repackage the product and lead a new market. Faced with the risk of another business failure, he gambled on the new product – and won. What looked like luck was only taking an opportunity.

So now think about all the external forces affecting you. These are your opportunities and risks. List the top two or three:

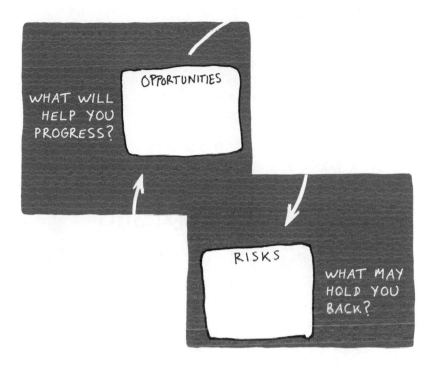

Equipped with clear and enduring *vision*, *values* and *goals*, and aware of the ever-changing nature of your *current position*, *opportunities* and *risks*, you are well placed to proactively chart the next leg of your journey. These are your **next steps**.

They are concrete actions, as measurable as your goals, but for the short to medium term. If your goals are two to five years hence, your next steps may be weeks or at most months hence.

So what are you going to *do*?

The other questions are servant to this master, a means to this end, the thinking before the doing. Ultimately, how you answer this question defines you as a leader. But how well you answered the first six questions determines the quality of this answer. What are your next steps? List them:

Andrew bet the company on the product change. But his first step was to convince his executive team colleagues to make the leap. So he undertook market research. This unassuming, single step reassured his team and proved to be the moment they got on board with the highly risky, and ultimately hugely rewarding, pivot.

These seven critical questions will help you create your *Leaders' Map*.

LEADERS' MAP

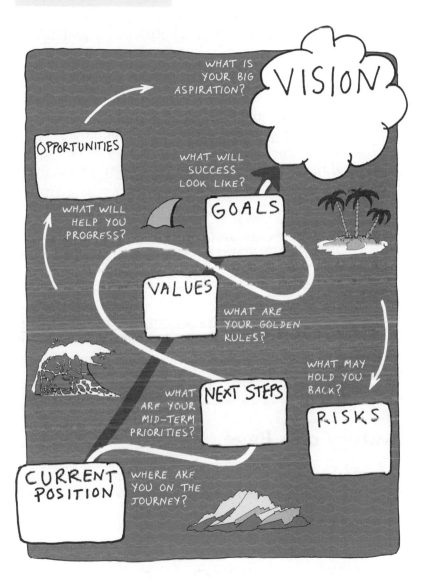

Keep Mapping

You have now created your storyboard of the future. Practise telling your story. Enjoy telling the story of where you are heading and others will engage.

Share it, but know that circumstances will change.

Your *Leaders' Map* articulates your view of reality now. It describes both your environment and your course. The dimensions and components of your map may remain stable for a period of time – but it won't be for long. This is not a fixed roadmap.

A call from a client tomorrow may change your options, a surprise resignation from your sales manager next week could alter the dynamics of your organisation, or volatility in the stock market next month may radically affect your profit outlook.

Remember that your vision, values and goals are your constants. They will help you to chart your course; everything else will change constantly. So you will need to be alert and continually reviewing your plan.

This is the process of mapping. But do it in pencil.

Strategy on a Page

As you have answered these seven questions, you've outlined your strategy. It may be easier to record this using our *Strategy on a Page – SoaP*.

STRATEGY ON A PAGE (SOAP)

LEADERS' MAP: 7 QUESTIONS	
VISION	WHAT IS YOUR BIG ASPIRATION?
VALUES	WHAT ARE YOUR GOLDEN RULES?
GOALS	WHAT WILL SUCCESS LOOK LIKE?
CURRENT POSITION	WHERE ARE YOU ON THE JOURNEY?
OPPORTUNITIES	WHAT WILL HELP YOU PROGRESS?
RISKS	WHAT MAY HOLD YOU BACK?
NEXT STEPS	WHAT ARE YOUR MID-TERM PRIORITIES?

LEADERS' MAP

PART TWO

Navigate

The art of life lies in a constant readjustment to our surroundings.

Okakura Kakuzo

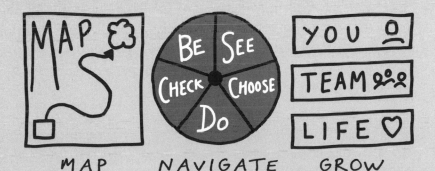

MAP   NAVIGATE   GROW

Time for Action

You have a map. Now is the time for action – to navigate to your destination.

You have worked on your strategy, now you need to make things happen. Almost as soon as you set off, you will face the critical test of the leader. Do you hold your course, or adjust slightly or, occasionally, drastically? This is the challenge of tacking and turning – of pivoting.

Former British Prime Minister Margaret Thatcher, seeking to establish her credentials as a strong leader, famously said 'The lady's not for turning'. But all leaders will need to tack and turn – to keep to their vision. Life has a tendency to throw you off course, so you need to pivot, readjusting your course to sail to your destination.

Anticipating the right moment to make a course adjustment is central to the art of leadership. Course corrections are needed to reach your destination.

As Jordan Seng says, 'You don't drift on target.'

This is the key challenge the leader constantly faces. Others will have their views, and many will offer you an opinion. But it's your call. Keep sailing on with favourable winds and risk hitting the rocks? Or pivot away and risk getting becalmed?

You will have some data, but never enough for certainty. It will be obvious in hindsight which decision is best, but you have to lead looking forward. Others can enjoy the game of hindsight, but leaders have no such luxury.

What are you going to do?

These moments of decision are the most important for the leader. They are pivotal.

Effective leaders not only train themselves to make the right calls, but they also teach themselves to spot a pivotal moment as it arises, and even anticipate when it may arise.

Navigating is about spotting the turns and making them.

When the leader *navigates*, everyone stays on track and everyone reaches the destination.

THE LEADERS' HELM

The *Leaders' Helm* is the wheel that will help you steer and navigate your way forward.

It has five key elements. Each element is essential for the leadership journey. If you master each of them you will navigate well. You will need to put your hand on each part of the helm frequently, just as a sailor constantly moves their hands around the whole wheel.

First, you need to **see the big picture**. To know where you're going you need to see beyond the confines of your situation. You've already looked at the big picture as you've charted your map. You've looked all the way from the horizon to your goals in the distance. You've looked left and right to see the opportunities and risks and those right under your nose. You've seen the big picture. But it can't end there. You constantly need to keep one eye on the whole picture.

Second, you need to **choose the right direction**. Looking at the bewildering options on the uncharted waters, you need to set sail in the best direction to your vision. It won't be a straight line – you'll have to tack and turn – but you've set your initial course. Keep choosing the right direction.

Third, you need to **do the right things**. Setting the course in one direction doesn't guarantee success. If you do the wrong things you'll end up off course. But do the right things and you will be heading towards success. Choosing the right next steps in your *Leaders' Map* starts the process of doing the right things.

Fourth, you must **check progress**. Analysing your current situation will quickly tell you how much progress you've made. You will need to keep on checking progress, especially as you tack and turn.

Fifth, and finally, **be inspired**. Above all, your vision should inspire you. You need inspiration to choose your next steps and act. If you are not inspired, how will you inspire those around you?

See, Choose, Do, Check, Be. These are the five key modes of the leader. When leading you will always be operating in at least one of these modes, and often in several simultaneously.

As you navigate your ship to your destination, you will keep tacking and jibing, pulling on the helm this way and that. So the helm rarely stays in one mode for any length of time. Steering needs constant adjustment, even if it is slight. The leader needs to be alert, adroit and agile to *See, Choose, Do, Check, Be* whenever needed. This is key to skilful navigation, to skilful leadership. Anticipate changing conditions, because the unexpected frequently happens. Life is not a straight line.

Focus 2

See the Big Picture

When you see the whole, you can stop reacting to events and start creating the future.

Anon

Look up. Look around. See the whole.

See what is above … in front … behind … beside … below … beyond … out of sight.

Enjoy the vista.

Assess the weather conditions. See what is going on in your world. What are the trends? Which way are things moving?

See things as they are. Spot the opportunities. Check the risks. See your way through.

Play with your head up.

The greatest sportspeople play with their heads up. They see the whole game. They seem to have more time than anybody else. They spot the opportunity to attack and also know when to defend. They see the right play at the right time.

Keep your head up, create space and time … and enjoy the game!

Let's now work through the following principles:

    2a Understand the Why

    2b Think outside-in

    2c Make the connections

    2d Look inside the box

    2e Take the long view

2a Understand the Why

People don't buy what you do, they buy why you do it.
Simon Sinek

Debt-free

'This is the wrong direction!'

It was early morning. I'd just changed jobs and was driving to my new office. I was lost in thought about the day ahead. Then, after 20 minutes, it dawned on me – I was heading back to my old place of work. Madness.

I was driving on autopilot. I'd climbed in the car and the car was taking me to where it had been going for the last five years. I wasn't driving … the car was!

It's easy to live life on autopilot – going through the motions, with the appearance of control, but not knowing where you're heading or why you're doing what you're doing.

Some time ago I was speaking with a colleague. He had a young family and put very long hours into his work. I asked what he wanted from life.

'To be debt-free.'

I asked why he wanted this. He answered, and then I asked 'why?' again. Finally, he said 'I want to create happy family memories.'

Then it dawned on us. Choosing long hours made sense to be debt-free, but perhaps creating happy family memories meant choosing to work *fewer* hours.

If we can't articulate where we're going and why, we're in danger of making poor choices. We've no basis to navigate. Everything becomes a priority.

I was in 'drive-mode'; my colleague was in 'do-mode'. Only after we addressed the *where* and *why* questions were we able to zig and zag back to the right direction.

You are the leader. So where are you going and why?

START WITH WHY

Simon Sinek, best-selling author of *Start with Why*, claims that:

> **Every** *organisation knows* **what** *they do. These are the products they make or the services they offer.*
>
> **Some** *organisations know* **how** *they do it. These are the things that make them special or set them apart from the competition.*
>
> *But* **very few** *organisations know* **why** *they do what they do.*

He analysed the approaches of a range of game-changing individuals and organisations such as Martin Luther King Jr, the Wright Brothers and Apple. He discovered that they all have something in common – they think, act and communicate in the same way. They all start with *why*.

Most of us naturally start to talk about *what* we do, then *how* we do it, and hope others 'get' *why* we do it. It is much easier to start talking to others about something that is concrete and easily definable like our everyday tasks.

Sinek says that in business, it matters less *what* you do, and more *why* you do it. He argues that ultimately 'people don't buy what you do, they buy why you do it'.

If you want people to follow you, you need to be clear about your 'why'.

Think

- Why?

Do

- Ask lots of questions. Ask people to clarify even if you think you understand
- Be prepared to *be asked* lots of questions. Don't worry if you don't have all the answers immediately – but do get back to them
- Watch Simon Sinek's original TED talk – *How great leaders inspire action*

2b Think outside-in

The magic formula that successful businesses have discovered is to treat customers like guests and employees like people.

Tom Peters

Mind reading

His store held the world record for the highest sales per square foot of any retail outlet.

Julian Richer opened his first electrical retail shop in London Bridge aged 19.

His company, Richer Sounds, competes very successfully in one of the lowest margin industries by providing expert advice. The stores are closed until midday every weekday so that the sales staff can learn the features of the latest flat screen TV, wireless streaming speaker or home cinema system.

Despite serving 12,000 customers a week, Richer responds personally to every customer complaint – and gets an average of just two. He believes that each customer contact really matters.

Richer Sounds now has over 50 stores across the UK, and they all have the same passion for customer service.

Your business model will be very different from that of Richer Sounds, but how do you put the customer at the heart of your business?

How do you look to your customers?

I wish I could invent a *CMRM* – a Customer Mind Reading Machine. The closest thing to it that is available on the market at present is some good, open questions, a pair of ears and a couple of legs to take you to your customer.

A critical part of seeing the big picture is to see it through your customers' eyes. Think outside-in. You'll learn more in a day talking to customers than in a week of brainstorming or a month of market research.

DARK SIDE OF THE MOON

How do you really get to know your customer?

The simplest way is to talk to them. Ask them what is important to them. Listen attentively and most customers will be able to articulate what their needs are. These are their *presenting needs.*

But how confident are you that they have told you all there is to know? If you stop there, you may only have part of the picture because that's all they have given you. They may have made assumptions about what you can offer and tailored their answers accordingly. They may not even have fully worked out for themselves what their most fundamental needs are.

If you base your offer only on what they have told you, you could limit your ability to meet their needs and also your aspirations for what you want to do for them.

Think of your customers' presenting needs as 'the light side of the moon'.

If your customer is the moon in this illustration, you are only seeing the part of the picture that is relatively easy to see, the part they have revealed to you. But to see the bigger picture you need to be able to see 'the dark side of the moon' as well – their hidden needs and interests. They need further exploration.

To reveal the light side of the moon you can simply ask your customer what their needs are and how you can help to satisfy them.

To explore the dark side of the moon and see the bigger picture of your customers' universe, ask them what *their* customers' needs are. If they can tell you what their customers' needs are, and how they are seeking to meet these needs, you will have seen the 'dark side of the moon'.

If you have also talked to their customers, then you will have definitely travelled to the 'dark side' and be in a great place to help them. That is 'outside-in thinking'.

Seek to help your customer succeed with their customers.

Think

- How well do you understand your customers' presenting needs (the light side of the moon)?
- What are your customers' customers' hidden needs (the dark side of the moon)?

Do

- Take a customer out for coffee and ask what their customers are concerned about
- Listen to your customer-facing colleagues, as they have their 'ears to the ground'. Train them and value them

2c Make the connections

If you want to go fast, go alone. If you want to go far, go with others.

African Proverb

A to B

I love a unique name.

Isambard Kingdom Brunel. You don't hear many children with those names nowadays.

Isambard was the king of Victorian engineers. He was a visionary and had daring. He had big, grand ideas. He has gone down in history for making connections from A to B in as many different ways as possible – railways, tunnels, bridges and ships.

During his relatively short career he achieved many world firsts. Brunel assisted in the building of the first ever under-river tunnel and the first propeller-driven iron ship, the *SS Great Britain*, which was, until the twentieth century, the largest ship ever built. He designed the Clifton Suspension Bridge, which went further and higher than any other bridge of its day. His designs revolutionised public transport and modern engineering. He achieved great things.

Yes, he had some spectacular failures, but Isambard Kingdom Brunel got results.

Reflecting on Brunel's unparalleled career, Professor Ross Peters argues that Brunel's genius lay primarily in his ability to get his ideas across to others. Without his ability to convince financiers and stakeholders to back him, as well as to inspire his workers, he would have accomplished little. Brunel knew he wanted to get from A to B, but he also needed to make great connections beyond his technical world. That also requires vision and daring.

We can easily get caught up in our own world. To make things happen you need to know who is in your 'solar system'. See the connections you need to make.

Who do you need to engage with to make it happen? How can you engage with them?

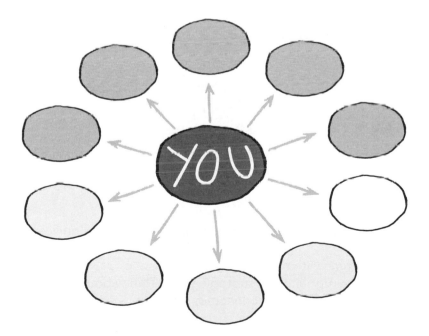

YOUR SOLAR SYSTEM

Identify your ten most important connections – five people outside (dark) and five inside (light) your organisation – and clarify each of their top priorities in each circle.

Most organisations describe the relationships and connections between people through their organisation charts. These tend to be a very hierarchical, fixed, wiring diagram with the CEO at the top and the most junior individual way down at the bottom. They can be useful, but they can be very constraining when you need to understand the real relationship dynamics of your role.

Who are the customers and key external stakeholders who will help you succeed?

Who are the colleagues, irrespective of their title and position, with whom you need to partner and bring on board?

What are the priorities, the agendas, of each of these individuals?

How can you best engage with them?

You could be far more creative and create your own solar system with planets of different sizes and distances from you to represent their importance and closeness to you.

Think

- Who are the most important people in your solar system?
- What are their priorities?

Do

- Contact those people you anticipate will grow in significance for you
- Invest time with them
- Play chess or another strategy game. Think about the whole and how things are connected, rather than just focusing on your next move

2d Look inside the box

I'll be more enthusiastic about encouraging thinking outside the box when there's evidence of any thinking going on inside it.

Terry Pratchett

The Santa Monica Warehouse

William Randolph Hearst was the most powerful newspaper publisher of the 1920s.

He invested a huge fortune in collecting works of art for his Californian home, Hearst Castle. He collected antiques and *objets d'art* from around the world and stored them in warehouses.

One day he came across the description of a rare piece of art in *Creative Arts* magazine. It was stunning! It was to become his next target, so he commissioned a number of agents to track it down. Months went by. Finally, his own agent returned and reported to Hearst that the item had at last been found.

Hearst asked, 'Where was it found?'

The agent replied, 'It was in your Santa Monica warehouse. You bought it years ago.'

When you look at your own situation and do a stock-check of your assets, it's important to value and celebrate what you already have. Appreciate your assets. Not only is it good for you, but it's mightily important for those who are working with you.

You may think you already do this. But try again. Noticing what you have takes conscious effort and choice.

Be careful of the 'new toy syndrome'. Sometimes when we think we are missing out on something, the solution is to be found inside the organisation. Make sure that you haven't overlooked or undervalued some asset that you already have. Look inside the box.

As you navigate towards your next opportunity or around a tricky obstacle, why not check that you haven't overlooked somebody who could really help you? Look a bit deeper and a bit wider.

Which 'assets' have you under-appreciated?

McKINSEY 7S FRAMEWORK

Consulting firm McKinsey developed a framework to 'look inside the box' of the organisation.

They identified seven characteristics that together help to describe an organisation. These labels offer a convenient way to explore what is going on in the organisation. Where the seven elements are aligned, McKinsey predicts organisational success. Where there are internal contradictions, expect to find a muddle.

The 7S framework covers both the so-called 'hard' and 'soft' elements of any organisation:

'HARD'	'SOFT'
STRATEGY: THE DECLARED PURPOSE AND DIRECTION OF THE ORGANISATION	SHARED VALUES: THE CORE VALUES AND UNDERPINNING CULTURE
STRUCTURE: THE RIGHT FRAMEWORK TO OPTIMISE THE ORGANISATION	STYLE: THE OVERARCHING STYLE OF LEADERSHIP
SYSTEMS: THE SUPPORTING PROCESSES FOR CUSTOMERS, PRODUCTION, INFORMATION, FINANCE, RESOURCES	STAFF: THE NUMBER AND TYPES OF EMPLOYEE
	SKILLS: THE SKILLS, CAPABILITIES AND POTENTIAL OF THE WORKFORCE

Both the hard and soft elements are critical to the success of any organisation. Leaders need to be strong in both areas, but invariably it is in the right-hand column where they can differentiate themselves most from the competition, or indeed most easily fall down.

Think

- When and how did you last 'look inside the box'?
- What are you currently looking for?
- Who have you recently overlooked?

Do

- Use the McKinsey 7S framework to review your enterprise. Propose some actions to make the most of what you already have
- Clear out a cupboard and give away a possession

2e Take the long view

Most people overestimate what they can do in one year and underestimate what they can do in ten years.

Bill Gates

The Nearly Man

It was scorching.

Napoleon was leading his army through the roads of France in the blazing sunshine. He turned to Berthier, his right-hand man, and said, 'I want my soldiers to march through the avenues of France in the shade.'

Berthier replied, '*Mon Général,* that will mean that we will need to grow trees and that will take 20 years.'

Napoleon looked at him and said '*Exactement* – that is why we must start today!'

An the Chinese proverb goes, 'The best time to plant a tree was 20 years ago. The second best time is now.'

Things take time to grow. You sow the seed and nature has to take its course.

Taking a long-term view involves thinking ahead and investing in something because you see the future benefits. It is also an attitude of not being distracted from your vision and goals or letting failures and disappointments along the way defeat you.

In 1939 Winston Churchill looked like a 'nearly man'.

Peter Drucker described him as 'a might-have-been: a powerless old man rapidly approaching seventy, a Cassandra who bored his listeners in spite of his rhetoric, a two-time loser who, however magnificent in opposition, had proved himself inadequate to the demands of office'.

In other words, he had shown great promise and potential, but had never quite made it.

Over the following five years, Churchill rose to his greatest challenge and became instrumental in saving the world from tyranny. In a 2002 BBC poll he was voted the greatest ever Briton – because of what he achieved in the years when the majority of people are retired!

Taking a long-term view is not just an intellectual exercise of thinking and planning, it is also about the choices you make and the actions you take.

We live in an age of the immediate, which can govern our thinking and doing.

We can, however, take a different perspective and 'play the infinite game, rather than the finite game'. A finite perspective focuses on only the immediate result, whereas an infinite mind-set is open to countless possibilities.

What is your long-term view?

THE KONDRATIEV WAVE

Nikolai Kondratiev was a Soviet economist during the time of Lenin. Sadly, he was one of the millions of casualties of Stalin's regime and was executed in 1938.

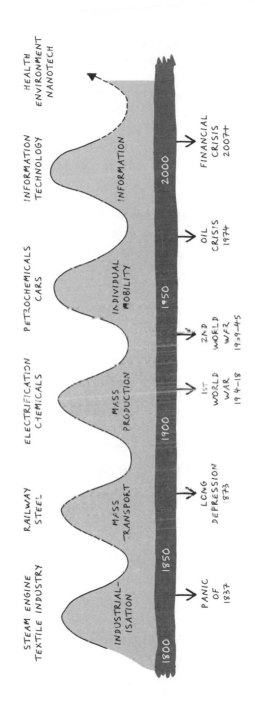

45

He is known for his theory that Western economies have long-term waves or cycles of boom and depression. He calculated these as around 50-year cycles, although there is some evidence that the cycle is accelerating to around a 30-year cycle, boosted by disruptive information technologies. But whether 50 or 30 years, each economic cycle has four stages, corresponding to the seasons: innovation and expansion in the spring, boom through the summer, recession in the autumn and depression in the winter.

While some economists challenge Kondratiev's long wave theory, for those of us who live in a society and economy where short-termism rules, it challenges us to think about the longer term.

Think

- What have been your best long-term investments, whether personal, professional, relational or financial?
- What have been the benefits for you and others?
- What is the long-term view for your business?

Do

- Invest in something with a long-term dividend that is very important to you
- Focus on quality growth and not growth for the sake of growth. You will then be more resilient to a downturn
- Plant a tree

Focus 3

Choose the Right Direction

The essence of strategy is choosing what not to do.

Michael Porter

'You can't have your cake and eat it.'

This made no sense to me as a child – what was the point of having a piece of cake if you *couldn't* eat it?! Now I understand the aphorism is about *keeping* your cake and eating it.

We tend not to like binary choices. We like to keep our options open. But we can't do that indefinitely. We have to choose, or choose to drift. You have to decide.

The '-cide' in 'decide' literally means to cut or kill off. 'Decide' is a killer word. Suicide, fratricide, pesticide and homicide are all 'killer words' – to kill yourself, a brother, an insect or another person. To 'decide', therefore, means to kill off or cut off all the alternatives.

Having worked across hundreds of organisations, we have found that the most successful know which routes to take and which alternatives to kill off.

The difficulty in making choices is killing off the other opportunities. But if you don't do that you'll abdicate responsibility for your future and just go with the flow.

For Focus 3, Choose the Right Direction, the following principles apply:

3a Start with the end in mind

3b Prioritise your priorities

3c Know your golden rules

3d Set the right goals

3e Communicate the course

3a Start with the end in mind

If something is important enough, even if the odds are against you, you should still do it.

Elon Musk

What's Your Ding?

Steve Jobs said his ambition was to 'put a ding in the Universe'. He did just that.

But when he was at college, he dropped out to drop in. He dropped out of his scheduled classes to drop in on classes he had no right to be in. In this unexpected way he became fascinated by, of all things, calligraphy. He later credited this passion and skill as the inspiration for the groundbreaking design at Apple.

He was acutely aware, long before his battle with cancer, that one day he would die. So he asked himself: 'If today were the last day of my life, would I want to do what I am about to do today?' If he said 'no' too many times, he chose to change something. He credited this philosophy with helping him make the big choices in his life.

Whatever you are doing now is the result of choices you have made – whether they were conscious or unconscious. We all face pressures that constrain us, some more than others. Ultimately, how we respond to those pressures is our choice.

Steve Jobs urged people not to live other people's lives, but choose their own. Don't waste your life living other people's lives, not even Steve Jobs'.

What is your ding? What choices will you make to make it happen?

If this were to be the last day of your life, would you want to do what you are about to do? Start with the end in mind.

CHECK YOUR VISION

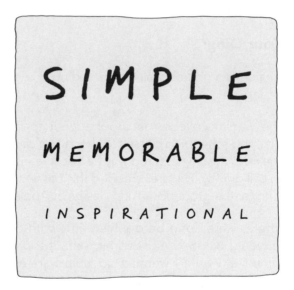

A good definition of vision is 'a compelling picture of what could be and should be'. What is your preferred picture of the future?

I was the business planning manager for UK retailer Woolworths in the 1990s, about ten years before it went bust. In my defence I hadn't read this book! My team developed the Woolworths' vision, which was to be 'the nation's low-priced, convenient, mainstream choice and quality, helpful answer to a range of everyday family wants'. I remember this even now – but the problem was that nobody else could!

Here are some much better vision statements, which we can remember even though we didn't develop them:

Make poverty history – Bono's ONE campaign
Organise the world's information – Google
Up for good – JetBlue

We have talked about and developed vision with thousands of people and hundreds of organisations. Very few pass the vision test.

Every vision statement needs to have three qualities:

1. Simple

Is it simple?

Your vision statement is for everyone, not just the experts. It needs to be easily and quickly understood by those on the outside. You cannot include every detail or qualification. Your vision needs to be 'simplicity on the far side of complexity'. It may not be complete, but it communicates the essence or crux of what you are trying to do.

2. Memorable

Can you and, more importantly, others remember it?

The easiest way to check is to ask them whether they can repeat your vision back to you. It is better to have a vision statement that is memorable and incomplete than one that is complete and forgettable.

3. Inspirational

Does it stir you ... and others? Are people excited by it?

Is it big? Does it raise expectations? Does it have a sense of significance? Is it a compelling vision of what could be and should be?

Will you and others be prepared to make sacrifices to achieve the vision?

The Woolworths vision failed these tests. The others passed all three tests – and led to success.

One or two out of three is not enough. Your vision test must have all three. Invest the time now to get your vision right and you won't waste time later on things that won't help you get there.

Think

- Do you start with the end in mind? Would others agree?
- How do you make your choices?

Do

- Review your *Leaders' Map* vision. How simple, memorable, and inspirational is it?
- Ask your team 'What is our vision?' Do they all give the same answer?
- Get your eyes tested

3b Prioritise your priorities

The main thing is to make the main thing the main thing.
Stephen Covey

Too Broke to Manage

Do you have any broken windows?

In 1982, social scientists James Q. Wilson and George L. Kelling introduced what they called the 'broken windows theory'. They observed that in neighbourhoods where one broken window was left unrepaired, the remaining windows would soon be broken too. Residents' negligence of broken window-type decay suggests it is a low priority for the community. Eventually this could lead to more serious crime.

During his second term as New York City's mayor, Rudy Giuliani was determined to put the broken windows theory into action. Despite New York's infamous image of being 'too big, too unruly, too diverse, too broke to manage', he wanted to prove the city was, in fact, manageable. A dramatic reduction in crime in New York resulted when efforts were made to stamp out minor offences such as graffiti and accosting people for money on the street.

The same principle applies inside organisations.

This is evident when it comes to the values you claim to hold and the service levels and product quality you want to offer. Tolerating abuse of your organisation's values by top performers or senior people is a perfect way to undermine your priorities. Releasing new products that don't meet your quality standards has the same effect. Giuliani did not go without his critics of his 'zero tolerance' policy, but he did prioritise his priorities.

53

Of course you choose the priorities, and you choose to live by them. If you say that customer service is your highest priority, but don't address rude or poor customer service, people won't believe you.

Where are your broken windows? Prioritise them.

THE EISENHOWER MATRIX
URGENT
HIGH
③ DELEGATE IT
① DO IT NOW
④ DITCH IT
② DIARISE IT
LOW
HIGH
IMPORTANT

Everything that comes your way can be measured as urgent/non-urgent and important/unimportant.

The urgent should not normally take priority over the important. However, the urgent can often crowd out the important. Urgent things often have short-term deadlines or consequences if we don't address them. Therefore, urgent things grab our attention.

We've seen many individuals and even organisations where everything is urgent. They fail to distinguish the urgent from the important and develop a pattern or culture of reactive behaviour and firefighting. This means important activities, which might not have an immediate deadline, never get done or are addressed too late.

The Eisenhower Matrix, adapted above, provides a simple rule of thumb to increase your effectiveness and productivity. It identifies four options for anything that comes your way. The key is to think about both importance and urgency. The two most difficult options are 'diarise' and 'delegate'.

The best leaders block time in their diaries for important, non-urgent activities such as one-to-ones with team members, development reviews, wider reading, exercise, etc. If you don't diarise time, other activities will steal it.

Often leaders delegate tasks when they should delegate authority. If you delegate tasks, you get followers. If you delegate authority, you grow leaders.

The frustration with delegation is that, to begin with, it takes longer. As any parent will tell you, quality can suffer. The aim of delegation is to reduce your own activity to the things that only you, uniquely, can do.

Think

- Are you fully focused on your main thing?
- Which important things have you shelved because you have been fighting fires?
- Do you delegate authority or tasks?

Do

- Prioritise your priorities. Complete the Eisenhower Matrix for your activities today
- Do it again tomorrow

3c Know your golden rules

*Those are my principles, and if you don't like them ...
well, I have others.*

Groucho Marx

Mafia

Easy Eddie was probably the top earning lawyer in Chicago in the 1920s. He worked for Al Capone, the legendary Mafia boss. One day, he determined it was more important for him to pass on a good name, rather than money, to his son. He decided to turn state's evidence against Capone and testified about his tax avoidance. Capone was sent to the notorious Alcatraz prison. Easy Eddie knew it would cost him his life. On November 8, 1939, he was gunned down in his car.

Butch O'Hare was a top pilot in World War Two.

On 20 February 1942 the aircraft carrier *USS Lexington* was attacked by nine Japanese bombers. Butch O'Hare single-handedly shot down three planes and chased the others away. He was the first US pilot in World War Two to be awarded the US Medal of Honor. Some years later Chicago's airport was named after him.

Butch O'Hare was Easy Eddie's son.

Who we are in our jobs and with our family and friends will always impact on each other. Easy Eddie eventually chose to live by a value which cost him his life. He left a legacy of courage which endured in his son.

The lesson from the story of Easy Eddie O'Hare is that we choose our values, and upholding values is not always easy. What values are you known for in your day job? What values will you hold to your detriment? What adjectives might others use to describe you?

How are these values practically demonstrated in the decisions you make and the actions you take?

APPRECIATIVE INQUIRY

So how do you discover your own or your organisation's values?

We often assess situations as 'problems to be solved'. We ask 'What's wrong?' or 'What needs to be fixed?' or if we don't want to appear too critical 'What are the challenges?'

These questions start from an assumption that there is dysfunction or deficiency – something needs to be fixed or solved. *Appreciative Inquiry* was the first serious managerial method to refocus attention on what works and is excellent, the positive core, and on what people really care about.

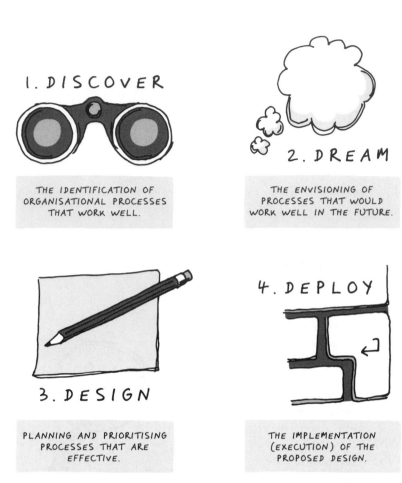

1. DISCOVER

THE IDENTIFICATION OF
ORGANISATIONAL PROCESSES
THAT WORK WELL.

2. DREAM

THE ENVISIONING OF
PROCESSES THAT WOULD
WORK WELL IN THE FUTURE.

3. DESIGN

PLANNING AND PRIORITISING
PROCESSES THAT ARE
EFFECTIVE.

4. DEPLOY

THE IMPLEMENTATION
(EXECUTION) OF THE
PROPOSED DESIGN.

Adapted from David Cooperrider www.davidcooperrider.com

The most common Appreciative Inquiry model is based on the four Ds – *Discover, Dream, Design* and *Deploy*.

The aim is to build – or rebuild – organisations around what works, rather than trying to fix what doesn't. Appreciative Inquiry practitioners convey this approach as the opposite of problem solving. Inquire into the 'exceptionally positive moments' with your team or the group you are working with. Here is an Appreciative Inquiry process that you can use with large or small groups:

1. **Discover** (in pairs)

   - Tell your partner about a situation or time at this organisation when you have really been performing at your best and producing great work. (5 minutes each)
   - What was it about the organisation that enabled you to produce that great work? (2 minutes each)

2. **Dream** (in pairs)

   - What key things do we want to take forward from these stories into our future? (3 minutes each)

3. **Design** (in main group)

   - Share the key themes or enablers with the main group from the *Dream* conversations. What elements are common to the moments of greatest success and fulfilment? These may be the unique processes or values that differentiate your organisation. (10–20 minutes)
   - Identify one story that represents the organisation's strengths when it is operating at its very best. Or (in groups of four) create a metaphor for your organisation as if it were operating at its very best every day. (20 minutes)

4. **Deploy** (in main group)

   - Pick a current project and discuss how you can bring these strengths to bear more consistently. (10 minutes)

Think

- How do you initiate conversations?
- What proportion of your conversation is focused on appreciating and building on strengths?
- What are your golden rules?

Do

- Use the *Appreciative Inquiry* process to highlight where your team is getting it right
- Make a list of all the airports that you have flown from

3d Set the right goals

I don't focus on what I'm up against. I focus on my goals and I try to ignore the rest.

Venus Williams

Chargeable Hours

'There's one crucial measure of your success around here', my new boss told me.

'Chargeable hours. All the other stuff is important, but if you don't deliver on your hours, you won't progress. Others may tell you that hours don't matter. Don't believe them. They aren't helping you. Your hours are critical.'

I had just joined a global consulting firm and I really appreciated having such a clear and measurable goal – the number of my hours each day that the company could charge to a client.

I noticed that colleagues who didn't meet their hours targets tended not to progress and left the company.

If I was working really hard and accumulating lots of chargeable hours, I loved knowing that the company was getting what it wanted from me and I was having a good year.

60

Ten years later, when I was leading a large part of the business, I would regularly review a spreadsheet with the hours of hundreds of consultants. It made good business sense. If a consultant worked 1,000 hours in a year and was charged to the client at $200 per hour, they had earned the company $200,000 in that year.

If a consultant had very low hours, it needed an explanation. And the answer was often found in lack of personal development or a reduced focus on clients. These activities were the best predictors of success in meeting performance targets. So they were also important goals.

It's good to track output measures. They define success. It's equally important to track input measures. They predict success.

The right goals meant that we always knew whether we were meeting, exceeding or falling short of expectations. If I consistently achieved them, it told me that I was heading in the right direction and progressing my career. My performance reviews could be challenging, but they had no unpleasant surprises.

4 DISCIPLINES OF EXECUTION

How do you manage the whirlwind most of us work in?

McChesney, Covey and Huling have developed the four disciplines of execution to help answer this question. The four disciplines are:

1. **Focus on the wildly important**

   How are you prioritising? The nature of the whirlwind means that the urgent often wins the case against the important. McChesney *et al* encourage us to focus on wildly important goals (WIGs).

   Look at all you have to do now. Can you identify one wildly important goal? It will:

- Answer the question 'If every other area of our operation remained at its current level of performance, what is the one area that will have the greatest impact on achieving our vision?'
- Be expressed in concrete terms (i.e. from X to Y by date)
- Be the thing of which you will say, 'of all the things we need to do, if we don't do anything else, we *must* do this', or 'if we do everything else but don't do this, we'll have failed'
- Be something you have control over (to a realistic degree)
- Be 'the battle that helps you win the war'
- Be important enough that you're prepared to spend 20% of your time on it
- Not be 'business as usual'

2. Act on the lead measures

If you're trying to lose weight, you need to measure your weight. But that's not enough. You need to measure how much exercise you're taking and how many calories you're ingesting. These are your lead measures, as they predict whether you are likely to achieve your goal. In the same way, client meetings were the lead measure for predicting success in the chargeable hours goal.

Identify the actions and behaviours that will lead to achieving your goal and then measure them. They must be things you have control over. They create the winnable game that is necessary to drive motivation and performance.

3. Keep a compelling scorecard

Having identified your lead measures, you need to be able to see instantly whether you're winning or losing. So you need a scorecard that shows the lag measure – are you achieving what you set out to achieve? But it must also feature your lead measures – are you doing the things you know need to be done to realise your ambitions? Are you winning or losing?

4. Create a cadence of accountability

McChesney *et al* prescribe weekly team meetings, separate from the team meeting that deals with the rest of the whirlwind. It allows peer-to-peer accountability on performance.

Did we do last week what we said we would do? How are we doing in the scorecard? What do we need to do in the next week to keep up momentum?

Then go and act on this, and come back the following week to account for your actions.

Adapted from *The 4 Disciplines of Execution*, by Chris McChesney, Sean Covey and Jim Huling.

Think

- What has been the most important goal that you have achieved?
- Why was it so important?
- How did you achieve it?

Do

- Use *The 4 Disciplines of Execution* to identify your 'Wildly Important Goal'
- Stick it on your mirror

3e Communicate the course

> *The single biggest problem in communication is the illusion that it has taken place.*
>
> George Bernard Shaw

The Paperweight

Monday 2 August 1943. John F. Kennedy probably thought his war was over.

He was the commander of a torpedo boat during World War Two when his vessel was rammed by a Japanese destroyer in the Solomon Sea. The boat was split in two by the impact and two sailors died, but Kennedy and ten of his men swam to the island of Nauru. Communication lines were completely cut off, and JFK and his fellow survivors had only coconuts and fresh water to keep them alive.

Six days later two Solomon Islanders, Biuku Gasa and Eroni Kumana, turned up in their dugout canoe.

The two groups couldn't communicate in the same language, so Biuku Gasa gestured that Kennedy send a message on a coconut shell. He inscribed:

> *Nauru Isl commander/native knows position/he can pilot/11 alive/need small boat/Kennedy.*

The two Solomon Islanders took the coconut and rowed their dugout canoe at great risk through 65 km of hostile waters to the Allied base at Rendova, enabling a successful rescue operation. Later Kennedy had the shell made into a paperweight, which he kept in the Oval Office.

Kennedy understood first-hand that you can be shipwrecked unexpectedly. The situation had radically changed. Their survival and progress depended upon his ability to communicate the course of action needed.

JFK crafted one of the most important messages of his life ... courtesy of a coconut. He learnt the power of a succinct, simple message that was crystal clear.

LEADING CHANGE

Keller and Aitken's McKinsey article *The Inconvenient Truth about Change Management* states that about 70% of change initiatives fail – so you need to know why your programme will be one of the 30% that succeed!

Leading change guru John Kotter investigated why change programmes succeed or fail. He identified eight stages to change, any one of which might be the source of the failure.

STAGE	LEADING CHANGE	SCORE YOUR CHANGE PROCESS 1 ◁ 10
1	**ESTABLISH A SENSE OF URGENCY** WHY SHOULD ANYONE WANT THE CHANGE? MAKE SURE ALL STAKEHOLDERS SEE BENEFIT IN THE CHANGE FOR THEM OR COMPLACENCY WILL RULE.	
2	**CREATE THE GUIDING COALITION** WHO WILL MAKE THE CHANGE HAPPEN? SUCCESSFUL CHANGE NEEDS INFLUENTIAL PEOPLE NOT JUST SENIOR PEOPLE. YOU WANT NO 'EGOS' IN THE TEAM.	
3	**DEVELOP A VISION AND STRATEGY** ONLY A CLEAR VISION CAN GALVANISE PEOPLE'S HEARTS AND DIRECT PEOPLE'S MINDS – CLARIFYING THOUSANDS OF DECISIONS.	
4	**COMMUNICATE THE CHANGE VISION** ONCE YOU'VE COMMUNICATED THE VISION, DO IT AGAIN... AND AGAIN. MODEL THE MESSAGE.	
5	**EMPOWER EMPLOYEES FOR BROAD-BASED ACTION** ALLOW A THOUSAND FLOWERS TO BLOOM! GET RID OF OBSTACLES TO CHANGE ENCOURAGE RISK TAKING AND PROVIDE TRAINING. CONFRONT THE PEOPLE WHO SAY IT CAN'T HAPPEN OR SHOULDN'T HAPPEN.	
6	**GENERATE SHORT-TERM WINS** PLAN FOR SMALL CHANGE THAT IS VISIBLE AND CLEARLY RELATED TO THE CHANGE EFFORT. REWARD EVERYONE INVOLVED. SMALL CELEBRATIONS FOR SMALL VICTORIES.	
7	**CONSOLIDATE GAINS AND PRODUCE MORE CHANGE** DON'T BE SEDUCED INTO THINKING YOU'VE WON THE BATTLE AT THIS STAGE – KEEP GOING. EXPAND CHANGE INTO MORE RESISTANT AREAS. HIRE, PROMOTE AND DEVELOP PEOPLE WHO CAN IMPLEMENT THE CHANGE VISION.	
8	**ANCHOR NEW APPROACHES IN THE CULTURE** IT AIN'T DONE UNTIL IT CAN'T BE REVERSED! KEEP MAKING THE CHANGE UNTIL THE NEW WAY SIMPLY BECOMES 'THE WAY WE DO THINGS AROUND HERE.'	

Reprinted by permission of Harvard Business Publishing from *Leading Change* by John P. Kotter © 1996 Harvard Business Publishing

While *communicate the change vision* is Stage 4, communication is essential to all eight stages. That is why communication is the most common reason given for poor performance during project debriefs and team reviews.

In our experience most organisations fall particularly short on step one – establishing *a sense of urgency*. Communication is essential to overcoming complacency and helping different stakeholders see that the current position cannot continue and that a new future is possible and desirable.

Think

- What are you currently trying to communicate?
- What would it take to triple the effectiveness of that communication?
- How do you communicate with people who 'don't speak the same language as you'? What would have happened to JFK if he hadn't tried?

Do

- Assess one of your projects in the light of Kotter's eight stages. Discuss your findings with your team
- Fear makes people freeze. Focus on the joy of change – on how people will benefit
- Read Chip and Dan Heath's *Made to Stick: Why some ideas take hold and others come unstuck*

Focus 4

Do the Right Things

Management is doing things right;
leadership is doing the right things.

Peter Drucker

What separates successful from unsuccessful leaders?

Doing the right things.

But what are the right things?

They are the things that are fully aligned to your values, your vision and your goals. If they are not in line … then don't do them. Don't be busy doing things, do the right things. It is your choice.

So how do you do the right things?

It's all about your mindset. It's about the way you look at each decision or action – each conversation, event, meeting, task or even your leisure time.

The Five Mindsets outlines five key ways to see and approach any decision or action. No decision or action is guaranteed to be successful, but the right mindset for a specific task greatly increases your chance of success. Your mindset dictates your behaviours. Your behaviours directly impact the outcome. And the outcome dictates your success.

You can view any decision or action in a *transformative, creative, proactive, productive* and, when necessary, *reactive* way.

These are *The Five Mindsets.*

You choose your mode or approach towards a particular decision or task. You are not just choosing what you do, but why you do it and therefore how you will do it.

The Five Mindsets will enable you to execute your strategy successfully. They can be deployed individually, by a team or by a whole organisation.

THE FIVE MINDSETS

TRANSFORMATIVE
DECISIONS AND ACTIVITIES THAT COULD BE
GAME-CHANGERS

CREATIVE
IDEA-MAKING OR ACTIONS THAT ENCOURAGE
DEVELOPMENT AND GROWTH

PROACTIVE
TAKING INITIATIVE AND BEING ENTERPRISING

PRODUCTIVE
DOING THINGS EFFICIENTLY

REACTIVE
RESPONDING TO PEOPLE AND EVENTS,
SOME OF WHICH YOU SHOULD SAY "NO" TO

In *transformative* mode, you will unlock the potential for an event to have a high impact. It could lead to radical change.

When you are being *creative* you are generating something new or stimulating development.

When you are being *proactive* you are taking the initiative. You anticipate the future and take action.

Being *productive* is about tackling important day-to-day responsibilities and getting things done.

You can, however, be driven by events and become *reactive* – responding to an external stimulus. Being reactive may add little value and may even be detrimental. So the reactive icon is a question mark, asking whether you should stop this activity.

But the reactive mode is not all bad. In life and leadership, we need to be agile and able to respond to frequent changes in circumstances, turning immediate problems into solutions.

You choose your mindset for every action or decision.

For example, if I buy flowers for my wife, I might choose to be:

- **Reactive** (she was rightly upset when I forgot to buy an anniversary card, so I'm hoping this will help)
- **Productive** (to make the house look more welcoming for visitors)
- **Proactive** (to remind her that it's our anniversary – she always forgets!)
- **Creative** (I've taken a flower arranging course)
- **Transformative** (who knows what impact this will have?)

It is the same activity – buying flowers – but with very different mindsets and therefore potentially different outcomes. You have the power to influence whether something will be transformative, creative, proactive, productive or reactive.

If your mindset isn't leading to success, choose another one!

All of *The Five Mindsets* are valid and useful. Different situations call for different mindsets. It's like having five hats for different occasions. Which hat do you want to wear for which situation? You choose.

Here are some examples in work and life. Of course, you may want to reassign the tasks to a different mode.

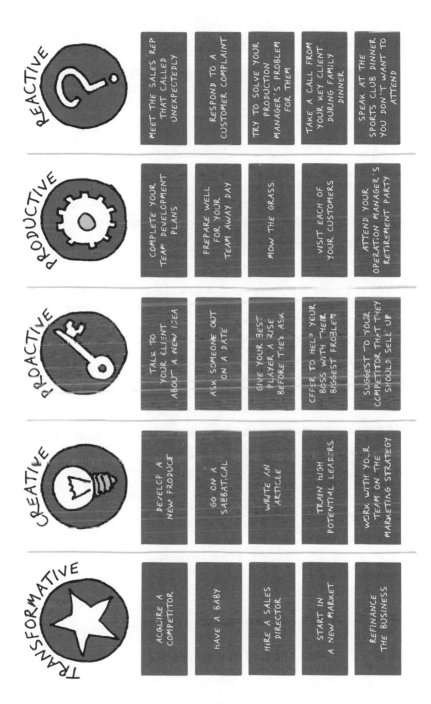

REACTIVE
- MEET THE SALES REP THAT CALLED UNEXPECTEDLY
- RESPOND TO A CUSTOMER COMPLAINT
- TRY TO SOLVE YOUR PRODUCTION MANAGER'S PROBLEM FOR THEM
- TAKE A CALL FROM YOUR KEY CLIENT DURING FAMILY DINNER
- SPEAK AT THE SPORTS CLUB DINNER YOU DON'T WANT TO ATTEND

PRODUCTIVE
- COMPLETE YOUR TEAM DEVELOPMENT PLANS
- PREPARE WELL FOR YOUR TEAM AWAY DAY
- MOW THE GRASS
- VISIT EACH OF YOUR CUSTOMERS
- ATTEND YOUR OPERATION MANAGER'S RETIREMENT PARTY

PROACTIVE
- TALK TO YOUR CLIENT ABOUT A NEW IDEA
- ASK SOMEONE OUT ON A DATE
- GIVE YOUR BEST PLAYER A RISE BEFORE THEY ASK
- OFFER TO HELP YOUR BOSS WITH THEIR BIGGEST PROBLEM
- SUGGEST TO YOUR COMPETITOR THAT THEY SHOULD SELL UP

CREATIVE
- DEVELOP A NEW PRODUCT
- GO ON A SABBATICAL
- WRITE AN ARTICLE
- TRAIN HIGH POTENTIAL LEADERS
- WORK WITH YOUR TEAM ON THE MARKETING STRATEGY

TRANSFORMATIVE
- ACQUIRE A COMPETITOR
- HAVE A BABY
- HIRE A SALES DIRECTOR
- START IN A NEW MARKET
- REFINANCE THE BUSINESS

So how do you choose which mindset to adopt?

By spotting the potential value of an activity to achieve your aims. The best leaders look for the potential in something, and then take action to realise it.

A decision, conversation or task does not necessarily have a prescribed value in itself. It is your mindset or behaviour, not the task itself, which creates the value.

Look again at the chart and imagine what your mindset would be if you reallocated each of the 'creative' activities to the 'reactive' mode. What would the consequences be?

Now try the reverse. Imagine tackling the tasks in the 'reactive' column in a 'creative' way. What might the outcomes be?

The most successful leaders consciously choose the right mindset to make the most of each situation. If you are not choosing, you are simply reacting.

Choose your mindset.

4a Be transformative

Boldness has genius, power, and magic in it.

Goethe

The Scrapbook

In December 1938 London stockbroker Nicholas Winton was planning a skiing holiday in Switzerland. He decided to visit his friend Martin Blake in Prague first. There he saw first-hand the plight of Jewish families facing Nazi persecution. Instead of going skiing he decided to help them. It proved to be transformative.

Winton found homes in Britain for 669 children, many of whose parents perished in Auschwitz. Eight trains reached London. The ninth did not. It was due to leave on 1 September, carrying 250 children – the largest number yet. That day Germany invaded Poland, and all borders were closed.

After the war he kept quiet about his exploits. The truth came out in 1988 when his wife Grete found a scrapbook in their attic. It contained lists of children's names. He then explained what he had done 50 years previously. An estimated 6,000 people across the world are descendants of 'Nicky's Children' to date.

He was knighted by the Queen in 2003.

His daughter, Barbara, said 'What he did in 1939 wasn't out of character. It was typical of the kind of impulses he has when he sees a situation and thinks it should be rectified.'

Nicholas Winton was a game-changer. He didn't have plans to change 669, and ultimately 6,000, people's lives; he was just prepared to act. He just did the right thing on one day. It wasn't out of character. The transformative outcomes just followed.

Look to be transformative. Explore ways in which you can be a game-changer in your situation.

CHANGING ROOMS

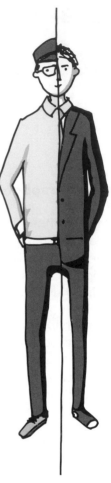

parkrun (www.parkrun.com) has transformed the world of running. Airbnb has transformed the holiday and short-term let market. It's easy to talk about and rationalise transformation, especially when we look back. It's more difficult to change your behaviour or lead transformation from the front within an organisation.

We have used *Changing Rooms*, developed by Willis Towers Watson, with thousands of people to help them experience change and draw out the principles of successful transformation.

Here's how it works:

Ask everyone to find a partner and for one person to be A and one person B. Ask A and B to turn back-to-back. Tell the Bs to 'change five things about their appearance'. No more direction needs to be given.

Once they have finished, ask them to face each other and ask the As to try to spot all five changes. Once some of the Bs start putting the five things back to their original state, ask them to go back-to-back again and ask the Bs to 'change a further five things about their appearance, to make a total of ten changes'.

When they have finished ask them to face each other again and for the As to tell the Bs what is different.

Let everyone know that the exercise has finished and you'd now like to review what this exercise teaches them about change. Ask the following questions of the whole group, starting with the Bs:

- *How did it feel at the start making a change?* The first change is often the hardest
- *What did most of the changes have in common?* They involved removing things. Most people instinctively think change involves loss and so they are anxious and fear change. People don't resist change if they believe that it will benefit them
- *How easy was it to spot the changes?* It's very difficult to spot the changes if you have not looked carefully at B before the exercise began. You need to know your starting position. If you don't know your starting position, you cannot measure change and progress
- *Did you get better at changing your appearance over time? Why?* Most people learn from others, often simply by copying what other people are doing. They learn to put new things on, e.g. they may make a hat out of a newspaper or borrow someone's glasses. The more often you change, the better you get at change
- *What happened after they completed the first five changes and A tried to spot them?* They started reversing all their changes. People find change uncomfortable and will revert back to how they were as soon as possible

- *What happened when you asked for 'five more changes',
  i.e. a total of ten changes?* There will be a strong sense of
  resistance in the room and often an audible groan! That's
  how change feels for people outside the inner circle who are
  designing and leading the change. It seems like a series of
  inexplicable changes from 'on high' requested in addition to
  a previous round of inexplicable changes

Think

- What has been the most transformative decision in your life?
- What would you like to transform in the future?

Do

- Watch the moment Nicholas Winton unexpectedly met some
  of the survivors he saved on the BBC's *That's Life* in 1988
- Make one change every day this week

4b Be creative

We don't grow into creativity, we grow out of it. Or rather, we get educated out of it.

Sir Ken Robinson

A Hundred Parakeets

Bill Thomas saw despair in every room. As a young physician in upstate New York, Bill Thomas took on his new job as medical director. His business was the care of 80 elderly residents who were physically disabled or had Alzheimer's disease.

The nursing home depressed him. So he tried to fix it the only way he knew. He did examinations and scans and changed medications. Little changed, except that the medical costs were driven up.

Then he looked at things differently. He diagnosed three plagues: boredom, loneliness and helplessness. His solution was to put life back into the home. That's what he did – literally. He put green plants in every room, organised a vegetable and flower garden and brought in two dogs, four cats and 100 parakeets – all contrary to the New York nursing home regulations. The fact that the parakeets arrived before their cages only added to the complete pandemonium.

Researchers found that prescriptions halved, total drug costs reduced to 38% of comparative facilities and mortality rates fell by 15%. Bill Thomas had looked at the situation differently from others. In the bleakest circumstances he saw the opportunity for life, and then creative ideas started to flow.

Why not discover your inner Leonardo Da Vinci and get your team together to discuss new ways of 'turning on the light'?

Think about your customers and your people. Be inquisitive. In what way would you like them to feel differently? What would bring life to them, and bring them to life?

Let your creative juices flow. Suspend early judgement on the ideas people generate – let them breathe and develop them.

CO-CONSULTANCY

Being creative involves using imagination and fresh ideas to create something.

What is the 'something' you want to create? It could be a new product design, a different way to approach customers, a better way to attract talent, a smarter way to take cost out of the business or an alternative format for the best end-of-year party ever.

We are all familiar with brainstorming. Co-consultancy is a structured alternative. It provides a similar approach for teams to work together to solve problems and create opportunities, but it does it in just 14 minutes.

One person in the group (the 'client') explains the issue to their colleagues (the 'co-consultants'), one of whom also takes responsibility to facilitate the process and keep time. It can be difficult for leader-types to follow instructions – but just do it on this occasion!

	PROCESS	RULES	PURPOSE	TIME
1	CLIENT EXPLAINS THE PROBLEM	CO-CONSULTANTS SILENT	CLIENT DEFINES THE PROBLEM AS CLEARLY AS POSSIBLE	2 MINS
2	CO-CONSULTANTS EXPLORE THE ISSUE THROUGH Q&A	QUESTIONS ONLY. CLIENT ANSWERS BRIEFLY	CO-CONSULTANTS UNDERSTAND PROBLEM CLEARLY	3 MINS
3	CO-CONSULTANTS OFFER SOLUTIONS	CLIENT SILENT, TAKES NOTES. NO JUDGEMENT ON IDEAS	CO-CONSULTANTS GENERATE AS MANY SOLUTIONS AS POSSIBLE	5 MINS
4	CLIENT EXPLORES SOLUTIONS THROUGH Q&A	QUESTIONS ONLY. CO-CONSULTANTS ANSWER BRIEFLY	CLIENT UNDERSTANDS POSSIBLE SOLUTIONS FULLY	3 MINS
5	CLIENT DECIDES ON AND EXPLAINS THEIR PLAN	CO-CONSULTANTS SILENT	CLIENT OWNS DECISION AND TAKES ACTION	1 MIN

Apart from stretching thinking, exploring imaginations and encouraging collaboration, it can remind a team of a few other important things:

- Clarifying the problem may take time, but it saves much more time in the long run
  Being silent can be hard work, but is essential for deep listening
- Having one person talking at a time will bring the best out of the quietest and often most reflective individuals
- Some discipline will encourage, rather than constrain creativity
- Teamwork can bring not only the best solutions, but also the quickest

Think

- What helps you think creatively? Are you more creative when with a particular friend, at a special place or away from distractions?
- If you had to start your own business, what sort of business would it be? How would you differentiate it from others?

Do

- Use *co-consultancy* with your team to unblock a seemingly intractable problem, or make the most of new opportunities
- Mobilise your most creative colleagues. Encourage them to innovate and share. Pay particular attention to the quiet ones
- Discover your inner Leonardo and plan something creative for this weekend

4c Be proactive

Ask and it will be given to you; seek and you will find; knock and the door will be opened to you.

Jesus

Potato Sacks

As a child she wore potato sacks.

That's because her family budget didn't always stretch to new clothes. Oprah Winfrey was shuffled between family members growing up, some of whom sexually abused her, and tragically she lost her son after a teenage pregnancy at age 14.

Despite this background, she managed to get a job at the local radio station when still at school and then won a full scholarship to Tennessee State University. During college, while co-anchoring on CBS, she was offered a job in Baltimore, Maryland. She had to choose between the job and graduating and she chose the job. Aged 20 she became the first black female news anchor.

She wasn't a great reporter and was soon fired from the job in Maryland. But with the help of her boss, she set up a talk show, called *People Are Talking*, aged just 22. She knew immediately after the first show that this was what she wanted to do for the rest of her life. She kept improving the show and eventually set up her own production company and talk show.

Oprah is, of course, now one of the most powerful and influential women in the world.

She pioneered the tabloid talk show, spawning a thousand imitations. *The Wall Street Journal* coined the term 'Oprahfication' to describe public confession as a form of therapy. She is credited with single-handedly bringing more than a million votes to Barack Obama with her endorsement of him in the 2008 election. *Forbes* estimates Winfrey's net worth at $3 billion, and she is the only black woman on the publication's list of the 400 richest people in America.

Oprah is known for saying she doesn't believe in luck. She decided to take the initiative throughout her life and career. She made and took hold of opportunities. That is being proactive. When things went wrong, people hurt or obstructed her, she wasn't defined or limited by those events. She 'adjusted her sails' and found other ways forward.

Another way of looking at it, in Oprah's own words, is 'Doing the best at this moment puts you in the best place for the next moment.'

All the great enterprises, whether in the corporate or social sectors, started with proactive people.

Sun Tzu said 'Opportunities multiply as they are seized.'

What does being proactive look like for you?

THE PARETO PRINCIPLE

The Pareto Principle is also known as the *80/20 Rule* and the *Law of the Vital Few*.

It simply, but profoundly, states that for many events, about 80% of the effects come from about 20% of the causes.

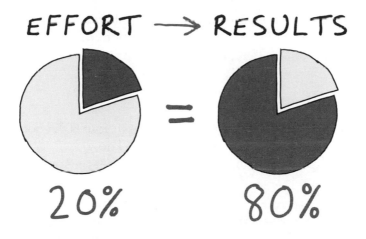

EFFORT ⟶ RESULTS

20% = 80%

So you might expect that 80% of your client platform will come from just 20% of your sales activity and that 80% of your sales revenues will derive from just 20% of those clients. If that is true, and our business experience says that is a valid 'rule of thumb', then it is a very powerful and practical insight.

The Italian economist and gardener, Vilfredo Pareto (1848–1923) discovered in the course of his research that approximately 80% of the land in Italy was owned by 20% of the population. He took the 80/20 principle to another level when he observed that 20% of the pea pods in his garden produced 80% of the peas! It can be applied to a range of other fields of activity:

- 80% of injuries in the workplace are caused by 20% of hazards
- 20% of patients use 80% of healthcare resources
- 80% of crimes are committed by 20% of criminals

How can you practically utilise the Pareto Principle to your advantage?

Be proactive with the 20% that produces 80% of the results.

Being proactive means creating or controlling a situation rather than just responding to it after it has happened.

Think

- What is in your 20% effort box? What is in your 80% effort box?
- Who is the most proactive person you know?
- What would you like to emulate about that person?

Do

- Initiate a conversation with someone who is important to you and find out what is currently most important to them. Suggest a couple of ways in which you could help
- Say to yourself every day this month, 'Be proactive!'
- Read the short but brilliant book by Dr Spencer Johnson, *Who Moved My Cheese?* (Vermilion 1999)

4d Be productive

Time is the scarcest resource and unless it is managed nothing else can be managed.

Peter Drucker

683,806 Hours

I recently asked a chief executive, 'What do you want?'

His immediate response – 'More time!' – will be echoed by many, probably including you and me.

Every day we spend 24 hours of our average 683,806 lifetime quota. The productivity and time management industry is booming: 'How can we do more in less time?'

Many centuries ago another senior executive was asked, 'What do you want?' King Solomon replied, 'Wisdom'.

For all our frenetic efforts to stop the grains from descending in the egg timer, we need to apply ourselves more to wisdom. Wisdom can give us perspective.

Solomon gave his perspective on time management and productivity when he wrote:

> *There is a time for everything and a season for every activity under the heavens: a time to be born and a time to die ... a time to plant and a time to uproot ... a time to mourn and a time to dance ... a time to search and a time to give up ... a time to be silent and a time to speak ... a time for war and a time for peace.*

Many of us live in 'urban time' and have lost a proper sense of the seasons – the natural time to do things. Wisdom is the discernment to work out the right time and season for everything. Timing is key to success – *when* do you need to do something? Then just do it!

Be productive – work smart and hard at doing the right things at the right time.

What is wisdom telling you about being productive today?

GETTING THINGS DONE

There are many productivity models available. Our take is based on our experience of applying and modifying a number of them:

Here's the process:

1. Collect all the 'stuff' that comes your way – your 'to do' lists, emails etc. Get everything written down in *one* place. It will release the stress of trying to remember everything.

2. Then make your first decision: Is it for you? Just because it was addressed to you doesn't mean you have to own it. If not, ditch it.

3. If it is for you, ask yourself 'What's the next action?' This insight has come from David Allen, the reputed guru of productivity. This question has released a thousand 'stuck' projects.

4. Can you do it in less than two minutes? Do it *now*.

5. Will it take longer? You have a choice. You can delegate it, or schedule it in your diary. Or you can still choose to say 'no thanks' and keep to your priorities.

6. Review your lists. Go through the loop of asking 'What's the next action?' on a regular basis.

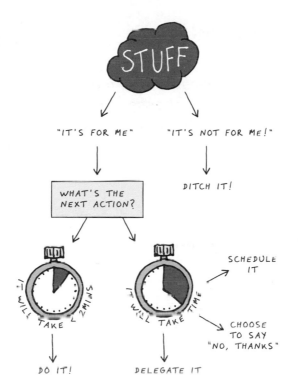

Adapted from *Getting Things Done: How to achieve stress-free productivity* by David Allen.

Think

- What stresses you most about the whirlwind you're facing?
- What isn't yours or could be done by others?
- How are you going to spend your time?

Do

- Refresh your productivity system
- Read David Allen's book *Getting Things Done*
- Take a device detox this Sunday. Don't even take your phone on a walk. Did the world stop turning?

4e Be reactive?

Between stimulus and response there is a space. In that space is our power to choose our response. In our response lies our growth and our freedom.

Viktor E. Frankl

The Marshmallow Test

'All you have to do is wait.'

The researcher was talking to a group of four to six year olds. The children were shown a marshmallow and told that if they waited for just 15 minutes before eating the marshmallow, they would then be given a second marshmallow.

Some waited and some didn't.

The research was being conducted in a US kindergarten in the 1960s. Follow-up studies over the years showed that there was a strong correlation between the ability to delay gratification in that nursery and various forms of success later in life, in terms of education and employment.

Not surprising, you say. But you and I face the same Marshmallow Test nearly every waking minute of every day.

We live in an age of massive information overload. In 1976 there were 9,000 products in the average supermarket; today there are 40,000. And yet most of our shopping is covered by 150 items. The noise screaming for our attention is increasing, and is becoming more immediate.

How many times a day do you check your mobile devices just in case somebody wants your attention?

There is a need to be 'master and not slave' to the information flow. Our success is also linked to our ability to delay gratification or just say 'no'.

The most successful leaders are 'self-leaders'. To stop being reactive be prepared to say 'no'.

What do you need to delay or say 'no' to today?

William Shakespeare said, '*Make use of time, let not advantage slip.*'

14 DAYS

14 Days challenges you to examine how you have spent your time in the last seven days and consider how you want to spend your time in the next seven days. This can apply to the whole of life and not just work.

Allocate your activities as to whether they are *transformative, creative, proactive, productive* or *reactive*.

Then estimate what percentage of time you have spent or want to spend in each area.

If this is done over a few weeks and months, expect your mindset to shift as you reflect, act, learn and reprioritise on not only what you spend your time doing, but also how you do it.

If time is allocated more towards productive, proactive, creative and transformative activities, inevitably there will be less space for the reactive. It will make it easier to say 'no' to distractions and reduce the opportunities for firefighting.

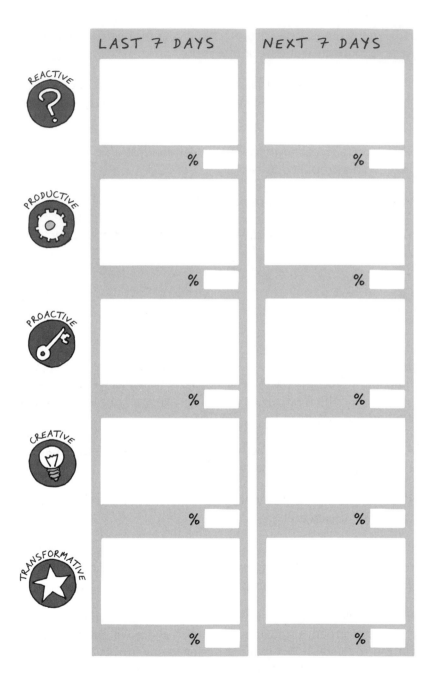

Think

- What is your natural mindset – reactive, productive, proactive, creative or transformative?
- How would you like to reset your mind?
- What do you need to say 'no' to?

Do

- Complete *14 Days* for yourself
- Leave some room for spontaneity. It could turn out to be creative or even transformative

Focus 5

Check Progress

We all want progress, but if you're on the wrong road, progress means doing an about-turn and walking back to the right road; in that case, the man who turns back soonest is the most progressive.

C S Lewis

C S Lewis hit the nail on the head. The most important question is whether you are heading in the right direction. Don't lose sight of that question as you look at the progress you are making. There is nothing better than to know that you are heading in the right direction, with the sun shining and the wind behind you. Celebrate the moment!

Checking progress also means asking 'Have we done what we said we would do and achieved what we said we would achieve?'

Don't react emotionally to criticism or disagreement – welcome them. Feedback is a gift. Be humble enough to know you may have missed something.

If things need to be fixed, don't just 'kick the tyres' and hope for the best. Leadership is not about having another good idea, but achieving results. Follow through is often the determining factor as to whether you will succeed or just miss out – in other words, fail.

But don't just look back, look forward. Check the weather conditions again. Demonstrate your agility to zig and zag at the right moment. Hold your nerve and take your people with you.

Adopt these core leadership principles:

> 5a Seek honest feedback
>
> 5b Get hard data
>
> 5c Adapt or die
>
> 5d Keep your focus
>
> 5e Expect accountability

5a Seek honest feedback

There is huge value in learning with instant feedback.

Anant Agarwarl

The Merchant of Death

How did the name of the man who invented dynamite become synonymous with peace?

He had some very unusual feedback, and he decided to do something about it.

Albert B Nobel (1833–1896) amassed a fortune by producing explosives. Nowadays this Swedish munitions manufacturer is best known for the Nobel prizes for literature, economics, sciences – and peace. The Nobel Peace Prize has been awarded to a range of luminaries – Barack Obama, Nelson Mandela, the 14th Dalai Lama, Desmond Tutu, Mother Teresa … and in 2014 to the youngest winner ever, 17 year old Malala Yousafzai.

When Nobel's brother died, a French newspaper mistook the death of his brother Ludvig for his, headlining his obituary 'The merchant of death is dead'.

'Dr Alfred Nobel, who made his fortune by finding a way to kill more people faster than ever before, died yesterday', the newspaper wrote.

What he read horrified him. He became obsessed by his potential legacy and changed his will to establish the prestigious prizes for peace and progress. It is a short case study of the power of honest, objective and timely feedback.

If you are to check progress, you will need people around you who will be prepared to be brutally honest. Seek honest feedback and don't stop seeking it. Be prepared to listen to your partner when they say 'You can't be serious!', or a friend who raises the question, 'Are you really sure?'

Who will give you the best view as to whether you are on course?

ENGAGEMENT INDEX

Many organisations use engagement surveys as a source of feedback or as an organisational health check. Numerous studies have shown that companies with higher engagement among their staff outperform their peers.

The eight questions in the engagement survey below assess the consistent drivers of employee engagement. Notice that money or pay do not feature.

Dan Pink in his book *Drive* argues that we are motivated by autonomy, mastery and purpose, and not money. He even shows how bonuses and incentive programmes can reduce motivation.

The questions address Pink's three core motivations. People are motivated by:

- Their opinions making a difference (autonomy – question 8)
- Getting better and improving their skills (mastery – questions 4 and 6)
- Having a clear line of sight from their jobs to the vision of the organisation (purpose – questions 1 and 2)

Your relationship with your boss or manager (question 3) is the single question in employee surveys around the world that

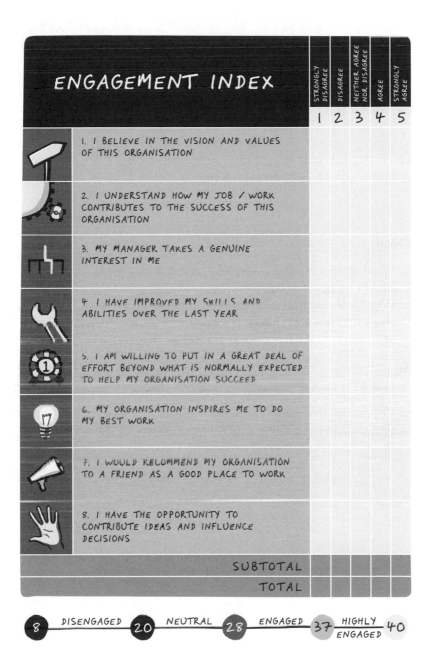

ENGAGEMENT INDEX	STRONGLY DISAGREE	DISAGREE	NEITHER AGREE NOR DISAGREE	AGREE	STRONGLY AGREE
	1	2	3	4	5
1. I BELIEVE IN THE VISION AND VALUES OF THIS ORGANISATION					
2. I UNDERSTAND HOW MY JOB / WORK CONTRIBUTES TO THE SUCCESS OF THIS ORGANISATION					
3. MY MANAGER TAKES A GENUINE INTEREST IN ME					
4. I HAVE IMPROVED MY SKILLS AND ABILITIES OVER THE LAST YEAR					
5. I AM WILLING TO PUT IN A GREAT DEAL OF EFFORT BEYOND WHAT IS NORMALLY EXPECTED TO HELP MY ORGANISATION SUCCEED					
6. MY ORGANISATION INSPIRES ME TO DO MY BEST WORK					
7. I WOULD RECOMMEND MY ORGANISATION TO A FRIEND AS A GOOD PLACE TO WORK					
8. I HAVE THE OPPORTUNITY TO CONTRIBUTE IDEAS AND INFLUENCE DECISIONS					
SUBTOTAL					
TOTAL					

8 — DISENGAGED — 20 — NEUTRAL — 28 — ENGAGED — 37 — HIGHLY ENGAGED — 40

correlates most closely to high individual engagement. Highly engaged employees tend to have good relationships with their managers. When they don't, they typically have low engagement and look around for other opportunities. A poor relationship with the boss is the main reason why people leave an organisation.

A willingness to go 'above and beyond' (question 5) and advocate for your place of work (question 7) are the final indicators of a highly engaged worker.

Think

- What is the number one skill you are currently developing based on recent feedback?
- What are your own scores in the index?
- How do you think your team members would score themselves?

Do

- Ask your team to complete the survey
- Act on the evidence
- Watch Dan Pink's *The surprising truth about what motivates us* on YouTube

5b Get hard data

Facts are facts and will not disappear on account of your likes.

Jawaharlal Nehru

Best Attendance

My daughter is a very talented footballer and all-round sports person.

It was a source of constant annoyance to me that her school sporting fixtures were cancelled at the slightest sign of bad weather. Yet her school had the best attendance and punctuality record in London. If she missed one day of school and I did not phone in or email with the reason, we received a letter to our home reminding us of our legal duty to get her to school. Friends even received phone calls after just one day's absence. However, she missed as many football matches as she played.

One day the teacher explained to me that sports activity wasn't measured at their school. In contrast, attendance and punctuality was pored over by the school leadership and local government. If a student was five minutes late or off school sick, it was recorded and reported.

The school's attendance and punctuality were nationally recognised. It was clearly communicated to prospective parents. The head teacher really cared about it. The school produced very good academic results from a mixed intake of ability, and they knew that children 'showing up' was vital to that performance. That's why they remorselessly measured and communicated their attendance and punctuality.

However, if a school football match or swimming lesson was cancelled, no-one knew. It wasn't recorded. They really didn't care.

What gets measured, gets done.

Make sure you measure the right things.

A BALANCED SCORECARD

There are two challenges with metrics and scorecards:

1. How do you measure less tangible, but important factors, such as commitment, loyalty, trust and purpose?

2. Does it tell you anything useful? Does it pass the 'So what?' test?

To address the first challenge, most organisations try to balance their scorecards by including non-financial measures. Most now measure their employees' engagement in their work. Just as a doctor would look at a range of scores to understand someone's health and vitality, we should look at a balanced scorecard for any organisation.

Even though you may recognise the importance of community and customer engagement and environmental impact, without real measures, their importance can be lost in comparison to compelling, clear financial metrics. Here are some metrics that can help balance your scorecard:

- Would you recommend us? (net promoter scores)
- Charitable giving as percentage of revenue or profit
- Diversity of leadership team
- Regrettable staff turnover (resignations among high potential employees)
- Job offer acceptance percentages
- Ratio of positive to negative stories in the press

Identifying 'lead' indicators (measuring things that lead to and predict high performance *before* the event), as opposed to 'lag' indicators (measuring things that demonstrate high performance *after* the event), is the key to the second challenge.

Sales is a lag indicator for retailers, but click-through rates from their adverts to their landing pages would be a lead indicator.

The level of whistleblower calls can be a lead indicator of a culture of risk or abuse inside an organisation. If employees feel less valued at work (as measured by regular surveys), this can be a lead indicator of higher turnover and retention problems.

Think

- What key metrics drive your decisions?
- What don't you know that you should know?
- What lead indicators should you measure?

Do

- Create a balanced scorecard to inform your day-to-day decisions
- Get hard data where it is missing. Be rigorous with the details
- See where things are getting better and spread that improvement – watch Hans Roslin's TED talks on data or read his book *Factfulness*

5c Adapt or die

If life doesn't go right ... go left.

Anon

Easy Lunch

The dodo was born to fly.

The three foot tall, 50 pound dodo bird was first glimpsed by Dutch settlers who landed on Mauritius in 1598. Seventy-five years later, the dodo was extinct. At some stage flying became too hard work and waddling took over. They probably read about the extinction of the ancient Archaeopteryx in their history lessons and said, 'It will never happen to us.' But it did.

Why did the dodo vanish so quickly?

Mauritius had changed radically and the dodo did not 'check progress'. Gone were the easy times when the birds could wander freely. They became easy lunch for Dutch sailors and were then finished off by their domesticated animals.

The message is clear. Adapt to the world as it is, not as it was.

Economies must adapt to the dynamic changes of globalisation and technology. Businesses should flex to the changing needs of customers. Even hiring new people requires conscious adjustments. That means doing things differently or doing different things and doing them quickly enough.

Once Chief Dodo started to see the numbers of Dutch settlers increase and the numbers of his dodo compadres decrease, he should have done something – quickly.

Adapt or die.

STAGES OF TEAM DEVELOPMENT

Bruce Tuckman argued that all groups go through distinct stages as they develop.

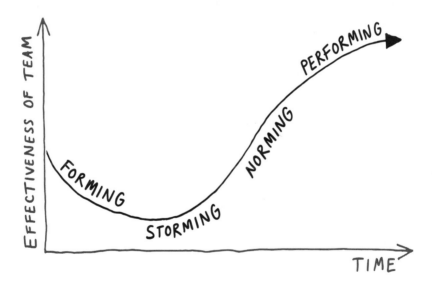

First, they 'form' as they come together. Soon they will 'storm' as they work out what needs to be done, who's responsible for what, how they're going to relate to each other and so on. As they come to agreement on these issues, they start to agree 'norms'. With these in place they can then focus on the goal in hand, and begin to 'perform'.

Performance will dip initially as the team takes its eyes off the ball to focus on the team issues. But it will shoot up as healthy norms enable the team to look up and out and focus on performance.

Tuckman argues that, while all teams go through this process, those that do so consciously and deliberately will be the most successful. Those that don't are the most likely to die.

Don't let things drift. Complacency is the greatest enemy of change.

Don't delay.

Think

- What stage of Tuckman's model is your team at?
- Diagnose your situation. Think of your business as a human body: how fit is it?
- How agile are you as a leader and as a team? Will you adapt or die?

Do

- Stretch your team with challenges for them to work on all together, e.g. how can we increase our customer satisfaction by X% and at the same time reduce costs by Y%?
- Rewrite and retell the story of the dodo as if it were your team and your situation
- Plan your next holiday … Mauritius?!

5d Keep your focus

Obstacles are those frightful things you see when you take your eyes off your goal.

Henry Ford

The Great Wave

Katsushika Hokusai liked change, but kept his focus.

He moved house 90 times and changed his name 30 times in his life. Eccentric he may have been, but Hokusai created the most famous image in all of Japanese art: *Under the Wave off Kanagawa* (c. 1830–1832), more commonly known as *The Great Wave*.

To the casual observer this iconic woodblock print is all about the huge, frothing wave. Take a second glance and you can see the boats that the giant wave is about to batter or consume.

Context, however, is everything. This is not a one-off piece of art, but part of a series that Hokusai developed – *Thirty-Six Views of Mount Fuji*.

The central point of this work is Mount Fuji. Take an even closer look at the print and you can see the wave 'spraying snow' onto Mount Fuji.

When things go wrong we tend to see the magnitude of the wave and lose our focus. Mount Fuji was the focal point of Hokusai's work, and he kept it right at the centre of his vision.

Keeping your focus is about knowing what should be the central point, even when distraction and turbulence are present.

What should be the focus of your attention and concentration as a leader when you are in the eye of the storm?

How can you prepare yourself?

WHEN THINGS GO WRONG

Everything seemed to be going so well, but then you got caught. You find yourself in the eye of the storm. Was it the wind or the waves that got you?

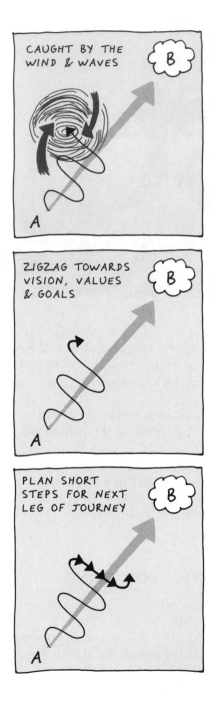

It doesn't particularly matter when you end up in a total whirl of fog, confusion and uncertainty and you haven't a clue which way you are facing. Direction, clarity and equilibrium have been lost – they have gone. It happens to us all and generally occurs when we least expect it. That's life.

When in a storm be quick to remind yourself of the essentials of your *Leaders' Map*:

1. What is my vision?
2. What are my values?
3. What are my goals?

They are your non-negotiables. Focus on them. Keep them front and centre in your thinking.

They will help you think more clearly when under pressure and re-establish what is important.

To ensure clarity and confidence on the next leg of your journey, reprioritise some short-term milestones that you can achieve. Make sure everybody knows why you have made the turn and chosen those particular tactical goals. Keep it simple and keep it straight. Once they have been achieved, then you will be ready to zigzag again.

Think

- What did you do the last time you got caught in major turbulence? What did you learn?
- What helps you to *Think Correctly Under Pressure* (T-CUP)?
- Check your current progress. Are you achieving what you promised? Are you on the right course at the right pace?

Do

- Expect and prepare for crises – they are a fact of life. But immediately apply the learnings, as crises shouldn't be a way of life
- If you need to pivot … turn now
- Listen to music that lifts and inspires you. Try Jenn Johnson's *You're Gonna Be OK* or Gustav Holst's *Jupiter*

5e Expect accountability

It is not only what we do, but also what we do not do, for which we are accountable.

Molière

The Perfect CV

It was the headhunter's dream day.

You opened the mail and found the person who could virtually do everything. Your wealthy client was looking to employ a military engineer. The curriculum vitae simply, but powerfully, described a breathtaking range of capabilities:

* Designs for adaptable bridge-building
* Vehicle manufacture
* Innovative ranges of weaponry
* Tunneling expertise
* New designs for ships
* Brilliant architectural ideas for public and private buildings

He also added that he could do paintings and a magnificent sculpture of a bronze horse for the client to wow all his houseguests!

The client was Ludovico Sforza, who in the early 1480s was ruler of the powerful city state of Milan.

The CV belonged to a certain Leonardo Da Vinci.

Leonardo didn't stop there. He went on to explain in his letter of application that if his master thought any of his ideas were impossible or impracticable he would be happy to demonstrate them in his park. He concluded the letter with 'I commend myself with all possible humility.'

Leonardo Da Vinci did not lack confidence in his capabilities, but he was acutely aware that he needed to demonstrate them. He expected to be accountable ... 'I said I can do it, I will demonstrate it to you, let you be the judge and I will accept the consequences.'

Being accountable is the willingness to be answerable for promises, choices, actions and behaviour – and to accept the consequences.

If we are not personally accountable, then it is unreasonable to expect others to be accountable to us.

As you check progress on how you are doing, it is crucial to hold yourself and others to account for success or failure. This requires:

1. *Objectivity* – look at the facts and weigh up changing circumstances.

2. *Self-examination* – look at yourself first with 'sober judgement'.

3. *Honesty* – don't fudge; say things as they are. Let people know what has happened and will be happening ... and do it well!

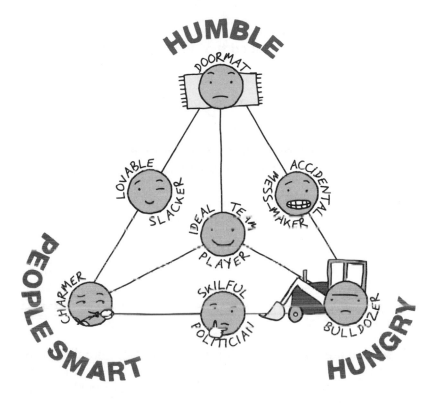

IDEAL TEAM PLAYER

Mutual accountability is a prerequisite of all effective teamwork. Patrick Lencioni, in his book *The Ideal Team Player*, describes the key attributes of those who are best suited to teamwork.

First, the ideal team player will be *humble*. It's not about them, their ego or their ambitions. It's about the team goal. But they're not self-deprecating – they know what they offer, and their commitment to the team goal means they will offer it.

They're *hungry* for success. They focus on the goal. They have the discipline to do the right things for success and the drive to overcome obstacles.

They are *people smart*. Lencioni describes this quality simply as 'smart', but we have changed the language to avoid confusion with intelligence. As they relate to their teammates, they see what impact their words and actions are having on others and can adjust accordingly. This is more about emotional intelligence, EQ rather than IQ.

Some people have only one of these qualities. Those who are only humble will be walked all over and are of less use to the team. People who are only hungry will bulldoze through other people to get what they want. People who lack both these qualities but are people smart are charmers.

Many people have two of these qualities. Those who are humble and hungry, but not people smart, Lencioni describes as 'accidental mess makers'. They mean well and they want success, but they don't see the effect they have on others, and can't adjust. They create messes wherever they go.

Those who are hungry and people smart, but not humble, have all the right attributes … to achieve what *they* want, but not to achieve the team goal. It's all about them. They are the 'skilful politicians'. They know the effect they have on others, and it's all calculated to get what they want, even it if looks like the team goal.

And then those who are humble and people smart are not in it for themselves. They know what effect they have on people and can adjust to get it right. But, lacking hunger, they use this to get along with people rather than get the job done. They are the 'lovable slackers'. The rest of the team loves to have them around; so much so that many will fail to notice they're not bringing anything to the party.

But those who excel in all three qualities will put their best forward for the team goal, will get the job done and will manage their relationships to greatest effect for the team. They are 'ideal team players'.

Think

- Which is your strongest Ideal Team Player quality? And your weakest?
- What can you do if you lack humility? Or hunger? Or people smart qualities?
- Who do you need to 'hold to account' in your team? What will be the consequences if you don't?

Do

- Ask your team to place themselves and their teammates in the model. Discuss the implications together
- In giving feedback to your team, focus on the facts, not your feelings. Be specific. Explain the situation clearly and reframe expectations for both parties
- Update your CV or your profile on LinkedIn

Focus 6

Be Inspired

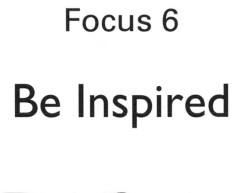

What you do makes a difference, and you have to decide what kind of difference you want to make.

Jane Goodall

Leadership thrives with inspiration, and dies without it.

The Oxford English Dictionary defines 'to inspire' as 'to fill (someone) with the urge or ability to do or feel something'.

It comes from the Latin *inspirare*, literally meaning 'to breathe or blow into'. It had religious origins of 'breathing in the Spirit'.

So whose responsibility is it to inspire your team? Yours.

Then whose responsibility is it to inspire you? Er … that would be you again.

Leaders can look to others for inspiration, but they are responsible for getting that inspiration. They can't expect others to do it for them.

So spend some time getting inspiration. It's not a self-serving activity – it may be the best thing you do for your team. If you are inspired, you're halfway to inspiring your team.

These five leadership principles are going to be fun! Follow them and be lifted up:

    6a Be a leading follower

    6b Pursue your passion

    6c Walk the talk

    6d Be courageous

    6e Make sacrifices

6a Be a leading follower

He who cannot be a good follower cannot be a good leader.

Aristotle

A Lone Nut

What transforms a lone nut into a leader?

Their first follower!

Former clown Derek Sivers has a great take on a three minute amateur clip of a crowd at a music festival. First one shirtless guy dances in an empty space with great enthusiasm and little technique. The cool kids sit around taking in the music, trying to ignore this geek. You can see what they're thinking – 'What a loser!'

Then another kid joins him, and together they dance with outlandish, unchoreographed and occasionally bizarre body moves. But they might as well be invisible.

Then another dancer joins them, then three more. Now they can't be ignored. A small cluster more and suddenly the dam bursts, and kids from all sides of the field come running to join in the crazy dance. The cool kids look at each other. If they don't move soon *they're* going to look like the losers.

Finally, even they join in, and the movement from one lone nut to a crowded field of dancers is complete – all in under three minutes!

Sivers shows it takes guts to be the lone nut dancing. But it also takes courage to be the first follower. It's what turns the lone nut into a leader. And it's an underrated form of leadership in itself.

In the most important thing you're doing, are you …

> … a lone nut?!
> … the first follower?
> … an early adopter?
> … part of the crowd, looking on?

Where do you need to be?

If you're the lone nut, leading where no-one is (yet) following …

1. Have the guts to do what you do – don't be afraid of ridicule.

2. Embrace your first follower as an equal. Bear in mind future followers will follow them, not you. They will show others how to follow.

If you've found a lone nut doing something good, says Sivers, 'Have the guts to be the first one to stand up and join in, and show others how to follow.'

DIFFUSION OF INNOVATION

How do you persuade others to accept your ideas?

How can they be diffused – spread among a wide range of people?

The *Diffusion of Innovation* is a theory that explains how, why and at what rate new ideas and technology spread.

The original concept of diffusion was first studied by French sociologist and criminologist Gabriel Tarde in the late nineteenth century. Gustave Le Bon advanced the ideas with his work on crowd psychology. The theory became popularised by Professor Everett Rogers in his 1962 book *Diffusion of Innovations*.

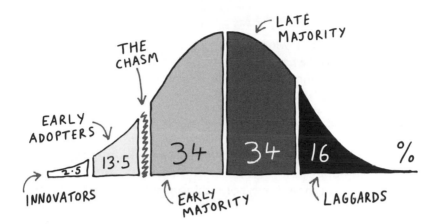

In the graph, the entrepreneur is well over to the left and the bureaucrat is to the right.

It indicates that it can be quite easy to win over a small number of followers. People who are naturally innovative or are early adopters will be open to your ideas, but then you hit the big chasm. How do you reach the vast majority – the 84% of your target population?

The early adopters are your potential champions. They play the crucial role of being the opinion leaders and evangelists. It's about them and not you. They are the ones you have to take some risks with.

If you don't invest in your close followers, don't expect your ideas to go any further

Think

- Who are you following?
- Do you model what it means to be a good follower?
- Who are the innovators, early adopters, early majority, late majority and laggards around you?

Do

- Watch Derek Sivers' three minute TED talk on *How to Start a Movement*
- Identify someone doing something right and start following them

6b Pursue your passion

And in the end it's not the years in your life that count. It's the life in your years.

Abraham Lincoln

Little Chance of Making Money

The idea came to her while she sat on a delayed train. It inspired her.

It was 1990 and Jo Rowling was a researcher and bilingual secretary for Amnesty International. She decided to put her idea for a story into writing. In 1991 she moved to Portugal to teach English. She met her first husband and had a daughter, but the couple split up so Jo returned to the UK and moved to Edinburgh. The next few years were tough – she was a single parent relying on state benefits and worked on the book while her daughter slept. Her finished manuscript was rejected by 12 publishers, and she was told that she had little chance of making money through writing children's books.

Rowling owes much to an eight year old girl. Alice Newton was the daughter of the chairman of publishers, Bloomsbury. Alice was given the first chapter of *Harry Potter* to read by her father. She loved it and immediately demanded the next chapter.

In June 1997, *Harry Potter and the Philosopher's Stone* was published. *Harry Potter* became the best-selling book series in history, generating over £500m in revenues. But J K Rowling had pursued her idea for seven years without encouragement or any hint of the rewards it would bring.

Ideas inspire.

Follow your ideas.

What will you pursue without guarantee of success?

Many people's inspiration is found outside their day jobs, but that can't be the case for the business leader – otherwise move over, as you are taking somebody else's place.

Inspiration, nevertheless, can run dry, and motivation can wane. Think again about what you believe in. Why not start to feed it and pursue it again? Then watch your energy levels increase.

THE FOUR CIRCLES

I've watched many friends and colleagues pursue particular careers simply because they pay well. I've seen others start out pursuing their passion, but give up when financial pressures increase. They may be musicians, artists or tech entrepreneurs, but there comes a time, perhaps when they start a family, when suddenly their career decisions are guided by money.

Career choices need to be guided by both passion and vocation. To determine your career, consider the following four questions:

1. *What are you really good at?* We tend to enjoy things that we are good at.

2. *What do you love?* What do you find easy to talk about? What do you often find yourself thinking about?

3. *What does the world need?* The world needs creativity, entertainment, education, sport, beauty, food, health, innovation, community and love. If the world needs it, it probably has a future.

4. *What can you get paid for?* What talents do you have that people will be willing to pay for?

Too many people consider only one of these questions, and often it's 'Where can I earn the most?' Bankers and lawyers often choose their profession because it pays better than any other. However, a 2014 UK report by the Legatum Institute showed that clergy had the highest job satisfaction, followed by farmers, healthcare professionals and teachers. Lawyers and bankers finished much lower down the satisfaction table. Many lawyers and bankers are very fulfiled, but if you pursue a vocation for purely financial reasons, without any passion for it, you may end up bored and frustrated.

If you can find a role or job that combines all four circles, you will have found your purpose. Work may still be hard, but it will be rewarding and meaningful.

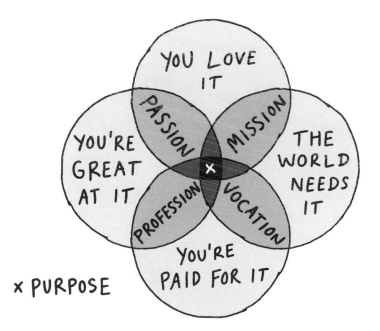

Adapted from an illustration of the *Ikigai* concept, created by Mark Winn in 2014.

Think

- Where do you, in your primary role, fit within these four circles?
- What could you do to combine your passion with vocation?
- Complete the sentence 'My purpose is ...'

Do

- Have fun – find people you enjoy working with and problems you enjoy solving
- Make decisions about your career that will move you to the centre of the four circles
- Read, or reread, *Harry Potter and the Philosopher's Stone*

6c Walk the talk

It's easier to act your way into a new way of thinking than think your way into a new way of acting.

Richard Pascale

Too Much Sugar

She was upset that her son was eating too much sugar. No matter how much she chided him, he continued to satisfy his sweet tooth. Totally frustrated, she decided to take her son to see his great hero, Mahatma Gandhi.

She approached the great leader respectfully and said, 'Sir, my son eats too much sugar. It is not good for his health. Would you please advise him to stop eating it?'

Gandhi listened to the woman carefully, turned and spoke to her son, 'Go home and come back in two weeks.'

The woman looked perplexed and wondered why he had not asked the boy to stop eating sugar. She took the boy by the hand and went home.

Two weeks later she returned, boy in hand. Gandhi motioned for them to come forward. He looked directly at the boy and said, 'Boy, you should stop eating sugar. It is not good for your health.'

The boy nodded and promised he would not continue this habit any longer. The boy's mother turned to Gandhi and asked, 'Why didn't you tell him that two weeks ago when I brought him here to see you?'

Gandhi smiled: 'Mother, two weeks ago I was still eating sugar myself.'

FOUR LEVERS OF INFLUENCE

The *Four Levers of Influence* model is the work of Scott Keller and Colin Price in their book *Beyond Performance: How Great Organizations Build Ultimate Competitive Advantage.*

They put out the challenge: if you want to influence people and make change happen, imagine yourself in the centre of the square. Put yourself in the shoes of the person you are trying to influence. Ask yourself the following questions:

1. Do you understand what is being asked? Does it really make sense?
2. Can you see the support that can help make it happen?
3. Do you have the skills and opportunities to make the change?
4. Are your leaders modelling the right behaviours?

All four elements are important and have to work in relative symmetry, but the last trumps the others. The one that is last on the list usually receives the least attention. By the time you get to it, your response may be 'Of course we are exemplars. Move on!'

Emily Lawson and Colin Price in their original *McKinsey Quarterly* article, *The Psychology of Change Management*, made the same point:

> *Most clinical work confirms the idea that consistent role models, whom the famous pediatrician Benjamin Spock regarded as decisive for the development of children, are as important in changing the behavior of adults as*

"I WILL CHANGE MY MINDSET AND BEHAVIOUR IF..."

ROLE MODELLING

"...I SEE MY LEADERS, COLLEAGUES AND STAFF BEHAVING DIFFERENTLY."

A COMPELLING STORY

"...I UNDER-STAND WHAT IS BEING ASKED OF ME AND IT MAKES SENSE."

SO STAND IN MY SHOES

SKILLS REQUIRED FOR CHANGE

"...I HAVE THE SKILLS AND OPPORTUNITIES TO BEHAVE IN THE NEW WAY."

REINFORCEMENT MECHANISMS

"...I SEE THAT OUR STRUCTURES, PROCESSES, AND SYSTEMS SUPPORT THE CHANGES I AM BEING ASKED TO MAKE."

Adapted from Scott Keller and Colin Price, *Beyond Performance: How Great Organizations Build Ultimate Competitive Advantage*

the three other conditions combined. In any organization, people model their behavior on 'significant others': those they see in positions of influence.

Within a single organization, people in different functions or levels choose different role models – a founding partner, perhaps, or a trade union representative or the highest-earning sales rep. So to change behavior consistently throughout an organization, it isn't enough to ensure that people at the top are in line with the new ways of working; role models at every level must 'walk the talk'.

If you want to influence, to inspire change in others, you have to 'walk the talk' first.

It has been said that 'inspiration is influence-za'.

Both influenza and inspiration are caught, not taught.

Gandhi chose to delay influencing the young boy until he could be the exemplar.

Think

- Remind yourself of a time when a leader wasn't 'walking the talk'. How did you feel and respond?
- Who has been most influential in your life? How did they model the right behaviours?
- How are you going to improve your influencing skills?

Do

- Choose a specific person whom you want to influence. Write down how you want the person's mindset to change
- Now empathise with them – put yourself in their shoes – to appreciate how they think, feel and see things
- Like Gandhi, check that you are walking the talk. When you know you are, then talk with them

6d Be courageous

Courage is being scared to death, but saddling up anyway.
John Wayne

Crocodile Barbecue

'Courage and kindness.'

These are the two parting words of advice that Bear Grylls gives to the 16 'normal people' he maroons for 45 days as part of the reality TV programme *The Island*. The islanders are left to source their own food and water on a small tropical island. There are arguments, fallouts and injuries. Some of them opt to leave, but most last the distance. They need courage to face tropical rain storms and endure extreme thirst and hunger. They typically trap and cook snakes and crocodiles. They also learn to trust, support and often forgive their fellow islanders.

Courage and kindness are critical to their survival and wellbeing. Bear Grylls clearly learned the importance of these through his own extraordinary life story. He undertook the notoriously gruelling selection course for the British Special Forces (21 SAS) and was accepted at the remarkably young age of 20. He was invalided out three years later after a horrific freefall parachuting accident in Africa, which broke his back in three places. It was touch and go whether he would ever walk again. However, only 18 months later and defying doctors' expectations, Bear became one of the youngest ever climbers to scale Everest, aged only 23.

Why is Bear Grylls so brave? In his 2011 autobiography *Mud, Sweat, and Tears*, just after he had broken his back, he wrote:

> *Sometimes it takes a knock in life to make us sit up and grab life … I have nothing ever to fear or worry about.*

Fear of failure, loneliness, commitment or the future can cause you to miss out on life. Confront your fears. Most of our worries never happen. Take a risk and be prepared to fail. Nothing ventured, nothing gained.

Be courageous. Be prepared to step out of your comfort zone. Why not take a risk and do something new today? What will it be?

GOLEMAN'S LEADERSHIP STYLES

Daniel Goleman identified six leadership styles springing from different aspects of emotional intelligence.

Each style has a different impact on the culture and results of an organisation. The best leaders do not rely on just one or two styles. Just as a golfer is proficient with a selection of clubs, the most effective leaders switch flexibly between the styles as needed by the situation. The best leaders may use all six leadership styles effectively within a single meeting.

The challenge is that some of the styles will be quite foreign to your personality. And it takes courage to step out of your comfort zone.

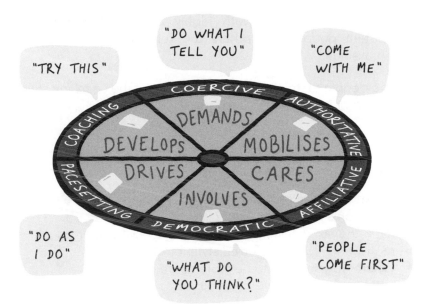

Leaders adjust their styles to get the best results.

In a crisis, or to kickstart a turnaround, the *coercive* style may come into play. In most other situations, or used as a dominant style, it will have negative effects.

When people need a clear vision the *authoritative* style of 'come with me' is very positive.

To heal rifts in a team or to motivate folk under stress the *affiliative* style creates harmony.

The *democratic* style builds consensus and encourages participation.

Pacesetting works best with highly motivated and highly competent people. For others the relentless drive can be demoralising.

Asking people to 'try this' is the core script of the *coaching* style and helps build long-term strengths.

Think

- In which situations do you see yourself using each of Goleman's leadership styles?
- Rank the six styles from your most to least preferred. How motivating is your preferred style for others?
- Where do you need to be more courageous?

Do

- Practise just one of your least preferred styles – in the right situation – until you are competent with it
- Read Bear Grylls' book *Mud, Sweat, and Tears*
- Do something courageous

6e Make sacrifices

I don't know what your destiny will be, but one thing I do know, the only ones among you who will be really happy are those who have sought and found how to serve.

Albert Schweitzer

Ferocious Focus

He took off his clothes.

What was he *doing*? Was he *mad*? Modesty preserved only by rough undergarments, he took a bowl of water and began to wash his friends' feet. *Kneeling!* It was humiliating. Person by person, foot by foot, between each toe, washing away the dirt and grime of the day.

Everyone knew the job needed to be done. But not by them.

In the ancient Near East it was the servant's job to strip down, and, shorn of any vestige of status or dignity, draw fresh cool water from the cistern and wash the feet of the guests. No-one with any self-worth would stoop so low. Even the more senior servants were exempt.

But with no servant present at this hastily arranged meal, who was going to do it? So they sat around, studiously avoiding the elephant in the room, growing ever more uncomfortable. Their feet were caked in the dust collected walking through the hot, rough streets of Palestine, their toes sore from the sand rubbing between them.

This practical service was also pregnant with symbolism. Twenty-four hours later, this leader would once again be stripped bare, sacrificially serving those who followed him in the ultimate way – dying for them. To lead them to a place they could not go on their own.

But that was the next day's work. For now there was dumbfounded silence. Finally he spoke. 'Do you understand what I have done? You call me your leader, and rightly so. I am. I have set you an example, so you also should serve each other.'

Leaders serve. But this was not a president proclaiming a desire to serve people from a marble hallway surrounded by power, money and the world's media.

This was a peasant leader, going by the name of Jesus, demonstrating self-denying sacrifice of the ultimate kind.

If you want people to follow you, be a servant leader.

GIVERS & TAKERS

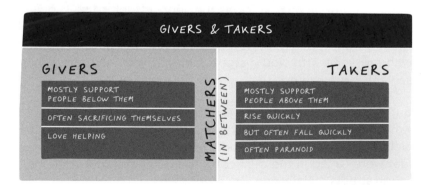

Organisational psychologist Adam Grant identifies three types of people – givers, takers and matchers, whom he describes as people who give as long as they get something in return.

He surveyed over 30,000 people in all walks of life to measure the relative performance of people in these three profiles. While the worst performers tended to be givers, so were the best performers. The insecure givers who allowed themselves to be exploited by takers were the worst performers. The self-assured givers who felt no need to assert their status, but who gave strategically for the better good of the team or organisation – and who were also capable of asking for help – were the best performers. They were also more likely to rise to higher leadership positions.

Self-interest and interest in others' wellbeing are not at opposite ends of a spectrum. Grant calls this mindset 'otherish' – almost the opposite of 'selfish' except it maintains a concern for self. Grant writes: 'Being otherish means being willing to give more than you receive, but still keeping your own best interests in sight.' This is different from matching. 'Matchers' expect to receive as much as they give. They give in order to receive. 'Otherish' people don't. They also know when to say 'no'.

Think

- Are you a footwasher?
- Are you asserting yourself over the right things or just asserting yourself?
- How are you currently serving others for the good of the team or organisation?

Do

- Rate your concern for self and your concern for others using the Adam Grant matrix
- Act decisively to sacrificially serve those you lead

PART THREE

Grow

Growth is the great separator between those who succeed and those who do not. When I see a person beginning to separate themselves from the pack, it's almost always due to personal growth.

John Maxwell

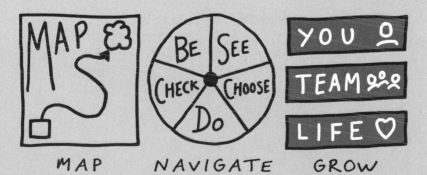

MAP   NAVIGATE   GROW

Growth Does Not Just Happen

Nobody welcomes the shock of having their life unexpectedly turned upside-down.

But go back to our earlier story about Andrew O'Shaughnessy. His experience of the unwelcome closure of the family mill unexpectedly became the source of the greatest personal growth in his life. Andrew traces the roots of his subsequent successes to that period of time and those experiences.

But the experience could have ruined him. Growth does not just happen. Karen Kaiser Clark says 'Life is change. Growth is optional. Choose carefully.'

Growth needs attention, nurturing and focus. Leaders who grow focus on three critical areas:

Focus 7 – You. Growing means first leading yourself before you seek to lead others.

Focus 8 – Your team. It means taking care of your people just as you take care of yourself.

Focus 9 – Your life. And it means thinking about your life as a whole and seeing every leadership venture as part of that bigger picture.

When the leader *grows*, everyone grows.

When the leader gets better, everyone gets better.

Focus 7

You

'Play to your strengths.'

'I haven't got any', said Harry, before he could stop himself.

'Excuse me', growled Moody, 'you've got strengths if I say you've got them. Think now. What are you best at?'

From *Harry Potter and the Goblet of Fire* by J K Rowling

To be the best leader you can be, you have to decide to lead as only you can. Lead from your strengths.

The best leaders know who they are – their strengths and weaknesses, their convictions and needs. They reject the debilitating thought that they have to become like someone else to lead well.

People follow authentic leaders. And people buy into the leader before they buy into the vision.

Having worked with thousands of leaders globally across diverse sectors, one of the notable features of standout, resilient leaders is their level of self-awareness and self-leadership. If you copy anything, copy that.

True success always begins with knowing who you are. So feedback from others is always a gift – even if apparently negative, and even if given with mixed motives. It comes with the potential to open up self-knowledge. And if part of the purpose of life is to know yourself, then feedback can help us achieve our life purpose.

Joseph Luft and Harrington Ingham systematised this process through what they called the *Johari Window* (so-called after their forenames, Joe and Harry).

There are things that I know about myself that everyone else is free to know too (for instance, that I'm a writer). This is the 'open area' of our lives.

There are things that I know about myself that only I know about me – the 'hidden area' of our lives. Were I to tell you, it would no longer be hidden, but move into the 'open area'.

THE JOHARI WINDOW

	KNOWN BY SELF	UNKNOWN BY SELF
UNKNOWN BY OTHERS	HIDDEN AREA	UNKNOWN AREA
KNOWN BY OTHERS	OPEN AREA	BLIND AREA

There are things about me that I don't know, but that others do – this is the 'blind area', since I am blind to them. I can't give you an example of this, but you may be able to! If we have any fatal flaws, such as arrogance, they will often be in our blind area. Few arrogant people realise they are arrogant; but everyone else does. But they may not all be negative – some very gifted people are the last to realise what a talent they have.

And then there are truths about me that no-one knows, not even myself – the 'unknown area'. These things may only be revealed when we experience new challenges, and end up saying, 'I didn't know I had that in me'.

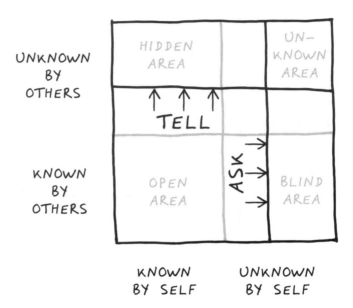

Wise leaders will extend the open area and address their blind spots. You can do that by *telling* (sharing more about yourself) and *asking* (seeking feedback from others about yourself).

As you reflect on YOU in the following pages, be prepared to challenge yourself more to:

7a Know yourself

7b Be teachable

7c Commit to your beliefs

7d Stay fresh

7e Be yourself

7a Know yourself

If you cannot tell the truth about yourself, you cannot tell it about other people.

Virginia Woolf

Make People Laugh

She makes me laugh!

Miranda Hart, creator of hit TV series *Miranda* and star of *Call the Midwife* is one of the biggest stars on British TV and winner of three British comedy awards. She has experienced tremendous success as an actor, film star and author.

She described her job as 'a weird one' where it's easy to be sucked into the fame game and a celebrity lifestyle. Her success has led to lots of other opportunities, busyness and the temptation to conform to the norms of her industry.

If you've ever seen or met her, you will know that she isn't like most TV superstars. She embraces her height and full figure and has built a career on being awkward and vulnerable, laughing at herself rather than trying to be fabulous. She knows herself and doesn't try to be someone else.

Miranda started to ask herself what her purpose is. Why was she doing her job? She concluded that her core purpose was 'to make people laugh'. She does this in a unique, rather British way. She enjoys bringing an element of escapism to people going through a hard time. She loves championing vulnerability and awkwardness for people who might feel like they don't fit in because, like her, they don't have the 'perfect family, Facebook profile or figure'.

She's comfortable in her own skin. She knows herself and doesn't try to be someone else. 'It's stopped me from burning out and helped me say no to some things. I won't go to that party because I need to do my job better tomorrow.' This quite simple realisation has helped her know what she should and shouldn't be doing.

Do you know yourself? Do you know your purpose? Are you comfortable in your own skin?

THE BIG FIVE

How can you understand yourself better?

Getting feedback from others, particularly people you trust, can provide important perspectives. You can also gain very powerful insights from using a self-assessment or psychometric tool. The most credible tools base their assessment on the *Big Five* personality traits.

1. **Extraversion.** Extroverts are warm and sociable, but the key point is that they gain energy from interacting with others. If you are an introvert you can tire from interacting with others and need space to replenish yourself. Highly extroverted personalities can be characterised as attention seeking or domineering. Individuals with low extraversion can be reserved and reflective, which may be seen as aloof or distant.

2. **Agreeableness.** While extraversion is about where people get their energy from, agreeableness concerns how well they get along with others. Highly agreeable people are trusting, patient and altruistic, but can be seen as naive or even submissive. Personalities with low agreeableness are often competitive or challenging people; they can also be seen as argumentative or untrustworthy.

3. **Conscientiousness.** If you have high conscientiousness you will be reliable, organised and like to keep the rules. You are prepared to delay gratification, have self-discipline and like to plan. But you could also be seen as stubborn or obsessive. At the other end of the scale, people with a low conscientiousness profile will see themselves as flexible and spontaneous, but can be thought of as sloppy and unreliable.

4. **Emotional stability.** Are you very calm and secure? Then you will be at the higher end of this scale. If you have a very high score you may be seen as uninspiring or unconcerned. A low score may indicate an excitable, reactive or even dynamic individual. It could also reflect somebody who is

nervous, pessimistic and unstable. This factor reflects how much your moods go up or down.

5. **Openness to experience.** Do you love new things and change, or do you prefer the familiar? People who like to try new things, to be vulnerable and have the ability to think outside the box usually score high in openness. Openness traits include being insightful, imaginative and having a wide variety of interests. Those with low openness gain fulfilment through perseverance and are seen as pragmatic and data-driven – and may be perceived as dogmatic and closed-minded.

If you know yourself, you will know where you are on each of the *Big Five*. There are no right or wrong personalities.

Be the best leader YOU can be. First know yourself, *then* lead others.

Think

- What makes you stand out?
- Rate yourself on the *Big Five*
- How does this profile show itself in your life and leadership?

Do

- Ask a couple of people who know you well to rate you. What do the differences indicate about how well you know yourself?
- Be prepared to laugh at yourself. You'll never be perfect – but you can be the best you can be
- Learn a new joke

7b Be teachable

Our acute need is to cultivate a willingness to learn and to remain teachable.

Charles R Swindoll

Grand Slam

She was the first.

No Asian tennis player had ever won a Grand Slam singles tournament … until Li Na.

And, despite winning the French Open title, Li Na appointed Carlos Rodriguez as her coach in place of her husband. Rodriguez helped her to the most successful years of her career as she became No. 2 in the world.

In most people's work lives, the more successful they become, the less time they give to developing themselves. But not Li Na. As she became more successful, she had *more* coaching for fitness, diet and psychology, as well as tennis.

Paul Annacone, who coached Pete Sampras and Roger Federer, two of the best tennis players ever, said of them both, 'No matter how good you are as a player … you need a trusted pair of eyes because your own eyes can't see if everything is on course. Those players have immense skills, but one of their biggest strengths is often that they are incredibly stubborn and a good coach can go in and handle that mentality.'

How teachable are you? Are you receptive to feedback?

If you are going to lead, you need to be learning and receiving – so stay a learner; be teachable.

Intractable, inflexible, stubborn, self-willed, opinionated, obstinate – these are all opposites of teachable. Not qualities that headhunters put at the top of their search criteria.

So what would you practically gain – in work and life – by being more teachable? How would others benefit?

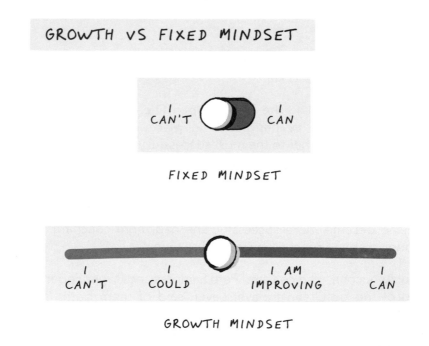

GROWTH VS FIXED MINDSET

CAN'T 〇 CAN

FIXED MINDSET

I CAN'T   I COULD   I AM IMPROVING   I CAN

GROWTH MINDSET

Your teachability will depend on your mindset.

How did you score yourself on 'openness to new experience' on your *Big Five* profile?

Do you think that talent and behaviours are carved in stone and don't change much once we reach adulthood? Or do you think that hard work, application and practice can help people learn almost any new skill or job regardless of their age?

Carol Dweck's research at Stanford University suggests that our response to this question is critical. If you have a more fixed mindset you will avoid trying new or difficult things and resist change. Conversely, if you have a growth mindset, you enjoy doing hard things because they stretch you and you learn something.

This has significant implications for education and workplaces. If you reward and praise ability, grades and success, that can create a fixed mindset. Students or employees with a fixed mindset avoid challenges because they may lead to poorer grades and failure in the short term. On the other hand, if you reward and praise effort, students and employees will often seek out new experiences and take risks. A growth mindset sees failure and risk as an opportunity to try new things, grow and learn.

Matthew Syed's book *Bounce* includes an extraordinary example of the growth mindset. He tells the story of the Hungarian László Polgár, who married Klara with the express intention, agreed before getting married, of proving that any healthy child can become a genius by rewarding effort. They had three daughters and let them choose the field in which they wanted to excel. The first daughter chose chess and the others followed, with each beginning her training at age three. Judit became the best women's chess player in history and has topped the female world rankings for decades. Susan, who became the second best woman in the world, was, at age 17, the first woman ever to qualify for the 'Men's' World Championship. Sophia was only the sixth best player in the world!

If you develop your own growth mindset, you can create a culture in which people embrace change and can excel.

Think

- How teachable are you? Would others agree?
- Where do you show evidence of a growth mindset, and where is there evidence of a more fixed mindset?
- Look back over the last few weeks. What have you measured and rewarded as a parent, leader or partner? Which did you praise more – ability or effort?

Do

- Grow. Begin with small steps. If you want to be less critical, then give a compliment; if you want to be healthier, then go for a walk
- If you want to learn more about having a growth mindset, then read Carol Dweck's book, *Mindset: The New Psychology of Success* or listen to her TED talk
- Learn new skills and sharpen old ones. Pick up a tennis racket or a trumpet. Join a language class or try hang gliding. Build a shed or write a song

7c Commit to your beliefs

Man is what he believes.

Anton Chekhov

The Mandela Challenge

I love films that make me think.

Justin Chadwick's *Mandela: Long Walk to Freedom* made me think. It chronicles Nelson Mandela's early life, coming of age, education and 27 years in prison before becoming President of South Africa. When Mandela was questioned about the possibility of taking revenge on those who had committed atrocities, he replied: 'I admit I want revenge, but I want something more than that … that is to live without fear and hatred.'

His response 'but I want something more' gives us an insight into one of the greatest leaders of his generation. He openly acknowledged his natural human feelings and responses to what had happened, but his overriding desire was for something better. He believed that there was a better way, and this influenced his choices.

Your beliefs govern your choices.

A belief is a conviction that something is true. Nelson Mandela believed that to live without fear and hatred was more important than the desire for revenge. This conviction governed his choice not to take revenge, but instead to take the path that would result in reconciliation. That and other choices reflected Mandela's character. His character is what made him stand out.

Your character as a leader will have a more telling impact upon your organisation, customers and people than your ability to manage profit and loss, launch your latest product or even pull off a stellar acquisition. Whatever is at the top filters down through the whole organisation, just as water flows down the mountain.

What you believe will be reflected in the teams and organisation that you lead.

Are you clear about your beliefs, and do you commit to them?

How do you respond to the Mandela challenge? What is the 'something more' that you believe in?

THE ONION MODEL

Shrek: *Ogres are like onions.*

Donkey: *They stink?*

Shrek: *Yes. No!*

Donkey: *Oh, they make you cry.*

Shrek: *No!*

Donkey: *Oh, you leave 'em out in the sun, they get all brown, start sproutin' little white hairs.*

Shrek: *No. Layers. Onions have layers. Ogres have layers. Onions have layers. You get it? We both have layers.*

Shrek, the ogre in the eponymous film, gives a great explanation of the onion model. If we want to understand an individual or an organisation, we need to peel back the layers to reveal their true identity.

The outside layers of the onion depict a person's visible characteristics such as hair, skin colour, clothing. The inside layers represent a person's unseen characteristics. One way to gain access to these unseen areas is to listen to people's stories. As they speak they reveal their hidden characteristics and we find out much more about what they are like.

Malcolm Gladwell, in *Blink: The Power of Thinking Without Thinking*, suggests that people make up their minds about new people they meet almost instantaneously.

Sometimes we do this very well. Years of experience allow us unconsciously to 'thin slice' and make accurate judgements about someone without even realising. Gladwell gives the example of John Gottman, a researcher on marital relationships, who can predict whether a couple will be together in 15 years with 95% accuracy after observing them for 60 minutes.

His accuracy is still very good if he observes them for only a few minutes. He has learnt to thin slice positive and negative emotion in a relationship. If there is too much negative emotion compared to positive emotion, divorce is a likely outcome. As we saw with Nelson Mandela, people's visible behaviours can reveal deep layers of character.

However, thin slicing and looking at the first or even second layer of the onion does not take account of prejudice and unconscious bias. We might not like to admit it, but we often better understand or prefer people who are similar to ourselves. What happens when we meet someone whose appearance and background is totally different from our own or who fits a stereotype such as the teenage mum or youth in a hoodie?

The trick is to peel away the layers to reveal the true beliefs that form the core of someone's identity. People often have not peeled away their own layers to understand their own identities. Thinking back to the Johari Window, friends and colleagues can do you a great service by helping you find out who you are.

Think

- What is distinctive about what you believe?
- How is that reflected in your choices and behaviours?

Do

- Encourage people to tell you their stories. Ask how the stories have affected and shaped them
- Listen carefully to people today. What are they revealing about their feelings?
- Watch *Shrek* again with your family and friends

7d Stay fresh

Whoever refreshes others will be refreshed.

King Solomon

34.2% Salinity

Lakes need water.

If a lake is not refreshed with new water, evaporation will do its job and the lake will shrink in size.

This is what is happening to one of the world's most iconic lakes, the Dead Sea, at quite an alarming rate.

The Dead Sea is fed by the River Jordan. The Jordan has shrunk from a considerable river to almost a trickle in places because of damming and irrigation upstream. The consequence is that the Dead Sea is gradually disappearing. The circumference has been reduced by 2 km since I first visited it.

This situation is not unique to the Dead Sea. But the Dead Sea is unique. Why?

First, it's dead. With 34.2% salinity it is ten times saltier than the ocean and uninhabitable for fish and animals, hence its unhealthy name.

Fresh water may still flow in from the River Jordan, so why is it dead?

Here is the second unique feature. It is the lowest point on the earth's surface. It is 430m below sea level and getting lower each year. There may be an inflow of water, but there is certainly no outflow, hence the very high buildup of salts and minerals. No water can flow out – there is no through-flow.

Timeless principles are at work here. If there is no inflow things will shrink, and if there is no outflow things will become stale and eventually die.

As an individual, if you want to stay fresh it is imperative to have a regular inflow. It is also imperative that you ensure that what you receive flows out to others. This is particularly true for leaders – from what you receive, others should be the beneficiaries, not just you. You have both to receive fresh input, but also to give out. Otherwise it is likely to die with you.

The best leaders stay fresh … and refresh others.

How can you stay fresh – physically, mentally, socially, professionally, and spiritually?

What are your inputs?

How do the words of King Solomon apply to you?

Press the refresh button today.

THE FLOW MODEL

Hungarian psychologist Mihaly Csikszentmihalyi was deeply affected by his experience of growing up during World War Two and seeing its devastating impact on the adults around him. He became gripped by the question 'Where – in everyday life, in our normal experience – do we feel really happy?' He wanted to discover how we can experience that more and more in everyday life.

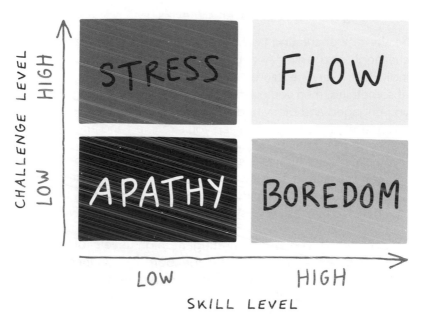

Adapted from Mihaly Csikszentmihalyi's Flow Model. (*Creativity: Flow and the Psychology of Discovery and Invention*).

His research led him to discover the conditions that led to happiness in daily life – a total focus on an all-encompassing task that leads to a sense of ecstasy, where:

- The challenge is immense but you know it's possible
- You instinctively know what you need to do next
- Time seems to disappear; and
- What you are doing is worth doing for its own sake

He described this state of happiness in the midst of daily work as *flow*.

But how do people get to experience this flow? Csikszentmihalyi's studies identified two factors. People experience flow when they are:

1. Operating at levels of challenge above their norm, and

2. Using skills at above-average levels.

So the task of creating flow becomes the task of increasing both challenge and skills. And because these are relative to each individual, everyone can experience flow. If you are highly skilled at something, then you need significantly more challenge to keep you engaged and motivated. Conversely, if you are less skilled, a lower level of challenge will keep you stretched and engaged.

If you experience high levels of challenge but do not operate with the commensurate skill levels, you may experience stress. With support, you will develop. But without support, you may burn out. You need to increase your skill levels to experience flow.

In contrast, if you are operating at high levels of skill but are under-challenged, you may be bored – so increase the challenge, perhaps by taking on more, starting a new role or leaving for new challenges. Low levels of both challenge and skill lead to apathy. Increase both.

Think

- In which aspects of your life do you regularly experience flow?
- Where are you operating well within yourself, bored or stressed? What would change this?
- What do you need to do to make yourself 10% sharper?

Do

- Avoid stagnancy. Identify an area in which you can increase your challenge or your skill
- Stay fresh by identifying one way that you can refresh others
- Learn how to pronounce Mihaly Csikszentmihalyi

7e Be yourself

Nobody does it better ... Baby you're the best.

Carly Simon

After School Closed

You are the best at who you are – but a poor imitation of others.

At about the same time that Bill Gates was sneaking out of his student bedroom to use his university's computer, my brother was holed up in my school's computer room after school closed. He was a brilliant computer programmer, but not great at passing exams.

His school continually gave him the message that he was a failure. But they failed – they failed to see or nurture his outstanding talent and passion.

Fortunately, my brother didn't try to be someone else. He carried on developing software in his spare time, and in the 1990s he set up a very successful internet software business. He became the best in his field because he created the field. No-one else can do what he can do.

You can't be whatever you want to be – but you can be great at being you.

Success is born from identifying your strengths, developing them and utilising them. You have unique strengths. You succeed when you play to your strengths. It is a case of 'playing your best cards'. Be crystal clear about what they are, otherwise they will be difficult to play.

You will know in part what you excel at because you know what energises you – but you may have missed something. Be brave and objective and get some feedback from others. Ask a couple of friends or colleagues today for their view of when you are at your best.

Be brilliant at who you are!

BEST CARDS

What are your best cards?

You can only 'play the cards' you have … but you can improve the way you play the game.

What are your three best cards?

What other 'good, but not great' cards do you have that you could play more wisely?

What card don't you have, but you need to succeed?

Think

- How can you play your best cards?

Do

- Identify three opportunities where you can activate your strengths in the next three days
- Who could provide you with the card or strength that you are missing? Go and talk to that person this week
- Have a game of cards with family or friends. Ask them what their top three cards are

Focus 8

Your Team

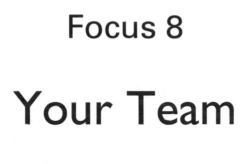

Before you are a leader success is all about growing yourself. When you are a leader success is all about growing others.

Jack Welch

Leaders must first lead themselves.

Then they lead others.

John Maxwell says, 'He who thinks he leads, but has no followers, is only taking a walk.' If you want to know whether you have any followers, look over your shoulder. Who's with you?

Your team is your crew. Without them you will not sail to your destination. You can't treat them any differently than how you treat yourself, except to treat them better. Serve them. In some senses they are an extension of you, so as you treat them well, you are benefiting yourself.

We are increasingly living in a 'selfie world'.

'I, me, my' language is in the ascendancy. A leader's language is littered with 'we, us, our'. It is a very different perspective.

Focus 7 was about developing your inner strengths and capacity to succeed with your aspirations and goals. Focus 8 is about developing the strengths and capacity of others to achieve your common aspirations and goals. The focus is on building their confidence and enabling their success.

Team members come with their own values and personality (character), their own abilities to relate to others (chemistry) and their unique skills, experience and capacity (competence).

Select and utilise your team members in this order of priority:
1. Character, because it is enduring.
2. Chemistry, because it can be difficult to change.
3. Competence, because it can be developed over time.

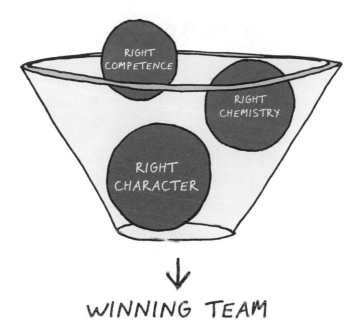

WINNING TEAM

Sir Ranulph Fiennes, the intrepid explorer who put together teams to cross the Antarctic and climb mountain ranges, said, 'Wherever feasible, pick your team on character, not skill. You can teach skills. You can't teach character.'

In Focus 8, Your Team, we will cover five key principles:

8a Choose the right people

8b Unleash people's talent

8c Appreciate your people

8d Grow your team

8e Build trust

8a Choose the right people

You don't train attitudes, you have to hire them.

Richard Branson

Livid

It still makes me livid even now when I think about it!

As a parent governor on the school board I was on the selection panel for the appointment of the new principal. There were two final candidates. The school had been well run, but now needed fresh direction and impetus. One of the candidates, who was dynamic and energetic, stood head and shoulders above the other, who was pleasant but ineffectual.

The traditional interview and selection process came down to a vote. The chairperson announced that Mr Pleasant had beaten Ms Dynamic by seven votes to two. I couldn't believe it.

They had opted for the easy, no threat, option … and they watched as the school went downhill for the next three years, during which the principal went off sick with stress. Consequently, we moved our children to another school within months.

Having the *right* people is the single biggest issue for any enterprise today. Knowing what to do is not the biggest challenge – finding the person to do it is. So find the right people. If you hire the wrong people at the top of an organisation, they can destroy it in no time at all. This applies to all key roles. Choose people you can trust. Remember that while competence can improve, character generally doesn't.

The right experience may qualify people to get to the starting line, but it is their character that will enable them to win the race.

Choosing the right people becomes your top priority as a leader. Look for winners, not starters.

EXECUTIVE MODEL (MERCURI URVAL)

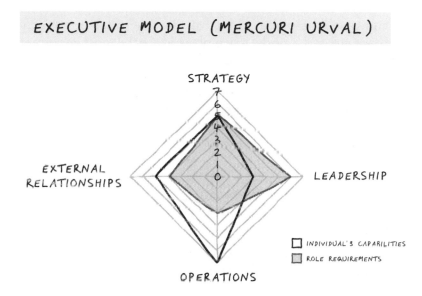

Choosing the right people may be the most important task for a leader, but it is certainly not the easiest. One of the biggest challenges is to define what is needed. You need to have a clear view of what is most important and what is negotiable. If this is not decided carefully you can end up searching for a 'five-legged sheep'!

Ram Charan, in his *Harvard Business Review* article, *The Secrets of Great CEO Selection,* highlights four qualities that great selectors of people demonstrate. Charan says, 'They work painstakingly to clarify the essential qualities needed to succeed in the job; they keep an open mind about where the best candidate will come from; they go deep to understand which candidate is the best fit; and they allow for imperfections in the chosen candidate.'

You need to be very clear about the demands of the role you are recruiting for and then rigorously assess the individual against those demands. Pay as much attention to this decision as if you were buying a car or a house.

Mercuri Urval, the global executive search and talent advisory firm, have created a model to weigh what are the most important capabilities for an executive role.

They weight the role against four dimensions – strategy, leadership, management and external relationships. Each role may have a different shape. They then assess the shape of the individual to check the 'fit'. This approach greatly increases the chances of getting 'round pegs in round holes'.

They define their dimensions as:

Strategy

- Set the purpose and direction
- Decide what is needed to succeed
- Clarify priorities

Leadership

- Communicate the vision and strategy
- Shape and influence the right culture
- Motivate people to engage and change

Operations

- Manage the key processes and resources
- Make things happen in daily business
- Drive and monitor performance

External Relationships

- Demonstrate credibility with external stakeholders
- Build trust-based relationships
- Influence others to 'buy' what you do

They describe every leadership role as a blend of these capabilities.

Think

- Look at the Mercuri Urval Executive Model. How good a fit is the individual for this specific role?
- What will the individual excel at? Where are they likely to have problems?
- What new avenues could you explore to find the right people for your team?

Do

- Draw the shape of your role and your capabilities. Identify the people who will cover your gaps ... and engage them. Hire to your weaknesses
- Consider sharing your skills at your local school or taking on another community responsibility

8b Unleash people's talent

In most cases being a good boss means hiring talented people and then getting out of their way.

Tina Fey

Talent Magnet

Talent shows have long been the staple diet for Saturday night TV viewing.

It is captivating when ordinary people do extraordinary things, particularly when we really don't expect it. They seem so ordinary and our initial expectations are low, but then they start to perform and ... 'wow'!

Seeing people thrive and smash expectations is one of the most important and gratifying aspects of leadership. Conversely, one of the saddest things is to see leaders overlook or constrain talent.

Christina was president of a pharmaceutical business unit. Her core skills were the ability to spot talent – particularly young talent – and then nurture it. In many ways, her team members were more brilliant than she was – it just so happened that she was great at unleashing their talent.

In working with Christina and her management team, it quickly became apparent that she had gathered together some naturally gifted individuals. Christina was a 'talent magnet'. They were raw in commercial experience and needed a few edges knocked off them and a bit of fine-tuning. Although Christina would not be the one who came up with the most original ideas or the best strategies, she had garnered huge respect and loyalty from the team. Christina exemplified Ken Blanchard's idea when he wrote, 'Help people reach their full potential. Catch them doing something right.' They were privileged young executives to be mentored in such a positive way.

Years later, those young executives are now spread throughout the industry in key leadership roles. Several of them have travelled further than Christina in terms of career and are CEOs of large businesses in different sectors. The common bonds and friendships continue to this day.

The reality is that each person has something that is unique, something extraordinary. It could be a great talent to ... listen ... create ideas ... sell ... organise ... care ... make things ... research ... empathise ... initiate ... compute data ... present an idea ... be loyal. The list could go on. The challenge for the leader is to spot it, nurture it and unleash it.

THE NINE BOX TALENT GRID

Does your organisation recognise the difference between performance and potential? Organisations can easily confuse performance and potential – at their peril.

It will impact on the decisions they make about their people and have substantial consequences. Performance relates to someone's ability to fulfil the requirements of the current role. Potential relates to someone's ability and capacity to fulfil the requirements of a different, often bigger role.

If you promote people purely on the grounds that they have performed well in their current roles, it could be a disaster for both the business and the individuals. Do they have the potential to meet the challenges of the new roles?

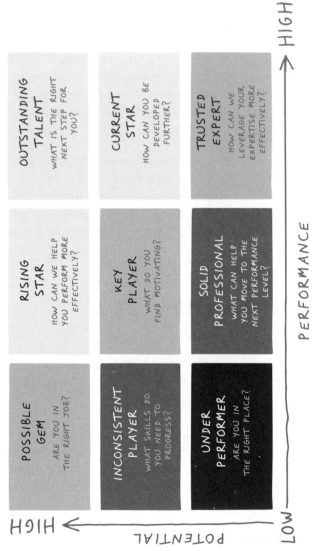

POSSIBLE GEM ARE YOU IN THE RIGHT JOB?	**RISING STAR** HOW CAN WE HELP YOU PERFORM MORE EFFECTIVELY?	**OUTSTANDING TALENT** WHAT IS THE RIGHT NEXT STEP FOR YOU?
INCONSISTENT PLAYER WHAT SKILLS DO YOU NEED TO PROGRESS?	**KEY PLAYER** WHAT DO YOU FIND MOTIVATING?	**CURRENT STAR** HOW CAN YOU BE DEVELOPED FURTHER?
UNDER PERFORMER ARE YOU IN THE RIGHT PLACE?	**SOLID PROFESSIONAL** WHAT CAN HELP YOU MOVE TO THE NEXT PERFORMANCE LEVEL?	**TRUSTED EXPERT** HOW CAN WE LEVERAGE YOUR EXPERTISE MORE EFFECTIVELY?

POTENTIAL — LOW → HIGH

PERFORMANCE — HIGH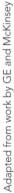

Adapted from work by GE and McKinsey

How do you spot potential?

- Look! Use your eyes to find indications that a person can, and has the appetite to, grow beyond their current position
- Take some risks and give people opportunities. Don't stop them falling over, but do protect them from a car crash

If you are looking for high potential, expect to see clear indicators that they:

- Have the agility to diagnose a problem and see a solution rather than just react to it
- Clearly communicate a way forward to others and can win them over
- Are personally highly motivated and resilient

The 'war for talent' has not gone away. In a fast-changing, competitive economy you need to have a strong grasp both on which individuals can secure strong performance and on who has headroom for growth. Of course, they may be the same people, but not necessarily.

Be clear what performance and potential means in your unique environment. Then objectively evaluate individuals against those criteria. Be open and straightforward with individuals. Have adult and constructive conversations.

Think

- What are the key indicators for performance and potential in your organisation?
- Where are you on the Nine Box Talent Grid?
- In what ways are you a 'talent magnet'? Why are people drawn to you – or not?

Do

- Assess your team against the Nine Box Talent Grid
- Draw up a simple plan for each person to accelerate their potential and performance
- Use the nine questions from the Talent Grid in your conversations

8c Appreciate your people

Praise works with only three types of people – men, women and children.

Anon

Valentines

I felt a bit embarrassed as I crept into my Atlanta office late one evening to put flowers on everyone's desks.

I'd just heard a very motivational talk about the 'power of appreciation'. With Valentine's Day fast approaching I decided to show some simple appreciation for everyone in my team and bought everyone some flowers and a gift card.

The speaker had emphasised the importance of the personal touch, so I decided to handwrite some letters. I wanted to capture the qualities and examples that I liked and appreciated about everyone, even the team members I found challenging. It took some time, but I really enjoyed doing something so positive and focusing on their good qualities and celebrating our successes.

Every team member came up to me and thanked me. Many sent handwritten notes back. A few years later, even after I had moved back to London, I saw that more than one of the team still had the handwritten letter pinned up above their desk.

This wasn't a natural action for me. But I knew that positive, genuine appreciation at unexpected moments is very motivating.

Jennifer Chatman, of the University of California, conducted experiments in which she tried to find a point at which flattery becomes ineffective. It turned out there isn't one!

Expressing appreciation, however, is much more than flattery and occasional gifts. Simple and genuine 'pleases' and 'thank yous' are normal courtesies that can easily be overlooked in challenging work environments.

So who are you going to thank today?

BELBIN'S TEAM ROLES

A successful team will have a complementary range of different personalities and skills. An effective leader will understand and appreciate each one and be the conductor of the whole orchestra.

What strengths should you be looking out for to develop your team?

Here are some suggestions of the strengths and weaknesses of people in a team setting, using Meredith Belbin's team model. Think about the people in your team and the role they typically prefer.

Willis Towers Watson surveys over a million employees every year. As we saw in the *Engagement Index* (see page 99), one question they ask consistently has the highest correlation to employee engagement – 'My manager takes a genuine interest in me.' There are two ways that you can show that interest and genuinely appreciate someone.

TEAM ROLE	CONTRIBUTION	ALLOWABLE WEAKNESSES
PLANT	CREATIVE, IMAGINATIVE, FREE-THINKING. GENERATES IDEAS AND SOLVES DIFFICULT PROBLEMS	MIGHT IGNORE INCIDENTALS, AND MAY BE TOO PRE-OCCUPIED TO COMMUNICATE EFFECTIVELY
RESOURCE INVESTIGATOR	OUTGOING, ENTHUSIASTIC, COMMUNICATIVE. EXPLORES OPPORTUNITIES AND DEVELOPS CONTACTS	MIGHT BE OVER-OPTIMISTIC, AND CAN LOSE INTEREST ONCE THE INITIAL ENTHUSIASM HAS PASSED
CO-ORDINATOR	MATURE, CONFIDENT, IDENTIFIES TALENT. CLARIFIES GOALS. DELEGATES EFFECTIVELY	CAN BE SEEN AS MANIPULATIVE AND MIGHT OFFLOAD THEIR OWN SHARE OF THE WORK
SHAPER	CHALLENGING, DYNAMIC, THRIVES ON PRESSURE. HAS THE DRIVE AND COURAGE TO OVERCOME OBSTACLES	CAN BE PRONE TO PROVOCATION AND MAY SOMETIMES OFFEND PEOPLE'S FEELINGS
MONITOR EVALUATOR	SOBER, STRATEGIC, DISCERNING. SEES ALL OPPORTUNITIES AND JUDGES ACCURATELY	SOMETIMES LACKS THE DRIVE AND ABILITY TO INSPIRE OTHERS AND CAN BE OVERLY CRITICAL
TEAM WORKER	CO-OPERATIVE, PERCEPTIVE AND DIPLOMATIC. LISTENS AND AVERTS FRICTION	CAN BE INDECISIVE IN CRUNCH SITUATIONS AND TENDS TO AVOID CONFRONTATION
IMPLEMENTER	PRACTICAL, RELIABLE, EFFICIENT. TURNS IDEAS INTO ACTION AND ORGANISES WORK THAT NEEDS TO BE DONE	CAN BE A BIT INFLEXIBLE AND SLOW TO RESPOND TO NEW POSSIBILITIES
COMPLETER FINISHER	PAINSTAKING, CONSCIENTIOUS, ANXIOUS. SEARCHES OUT ERRORS. POLISHES AND PERFECTS	CAN BE INCLINED TO WORRY UNDULY AND RELUCTANT TO DELEGATE
SPECIALIST	SINGLE-MINDED, SELF-STARTING, DEDICATED. PROVIDES KNOWLEDGE AND SKILLS IN RARE SUPPLY	CAN ONLY CONTRIBUTE ON A NARROW FRONT AND TENDS TO DWELL ON TECHNICALITIES

Used with the kind permission of Belbin

First, you can recognise someone's contribution. This is more than saying 'thanks'. It involves publicly and specifically recognising someone's contribution. Organisations often have recognition programmes and award nights, and these continue to thrive because of the power of recognition.

Second, you can appreciate and call out someone's qualities, gifts and talents. People want to be appreciated and loved for who they uniquely are. Belbin's research showed that a successful team comprises 6–15 people and needs someone to play each of the nine roles above. People typically have two preferred roles and generally don't like to have to play some of the other roles. If you understand your colleagues' preferred Belbin team roles, you will appreciate and understand what they can uniquely contribute to your team.

Think

- The attitude of a leader is contagious. What contagion are you spreading?
- Are you really interested in the people on your team? Can you name their major interests and the challenges they face outside of work?
- Do you and your team understand their Belbin team roles? Do you thank your Plant for her good ideas and your Team Worker for his diplomacy?

Do

- Write a handwritten note to each member of your team, thanking them for their specific contributions
- When congratulating colleagues, ask what helped them succeed – by understanding, you may uncover a hidden strength
- Take the Belbin Team Assessment with the rest of your team at *belbin.com*

8d Grow your team

If you delegate tasks, you'll build followers who only do what they're told. If you delegate authority, you'll build leaders.

Craig Groeschel

Manchester United

'You can't win anything with kids!'

Alan Hansen, the former Liverpool captain and new TV pundit, made his sweeping comments as Manchester United lost 3-1 at Aston Villa on the opening day of the 1995/1996 season. Manager Alex Ferguson had sold some very experienced players and packed his team with home-grown youngsters, including a 20 year old David Beckham.

On the very last day of the season they won the league title. Then they went on to beat Liverpool in the FA Cup Final! Hansen had to eat his words.

How did Ferguson do it?

He ensured that the club very carefully scouted and developed their pipeline of youngsters. They brought them through the youth academy and the reserve team. They provided mentors from the first team, and every now and then a senior player would play in the reserve team squad. Ferguson ensured that his experienced players brought on the youth players.

'A youngster never forgets the person or organisation that gives him his first big chance. He will repay it with a loyalty that lasts a lifetime', wrote Ferguson, in his book *Leading*.

United also developed a large, stable leadership team off the pitch, which allowed them to build the structures to invest in youth for the long term. During Alex Ferguson's time in charge, the other clubs in the Premier League went through 267 permanent managers. Chelsea alone went through 13 full-time managers.

Although they won with kids, it was a predictable return on a long-term investment. They kept on winning.

THE GROW MODEL

G GOAL – WHERE ARE YOU TRYING TO GET TO? WHAT ARE YOU TRYING TO ACHIEVE?

R CURRENT REALITY – WHERE ARE YOU NOW? WHAT ARE YOUR CHALLENGES AND OPPORTUNITIES?

O OPTIONS – WHAT POSSIBILITIES MIGHT ENABLE YOU TO ACHIEVE YOUR GOAL FROM YOUR CURRENT REALITY?

W WILL – WHAT CHOICE(S) ARE YOU GOING TO MAKE, AND HOW WILLING ARE YOU TO SEE THIS THROUGH?

The *GROW* model is used extensively in coaching, with applications for goal setting and problem solving.

It was developed by Sir John Whitmore, former racing driver and a pioneer of business coaching, in collaboration with Graham Alexander and Alan Fine.

The GROW method was influenced by Timothy Gallwey, author of *The Inner Game*. As a tennis coach, Gallwey realised that simply telling players what to do did not bring about lasting change.

Instead of shouting 'keep your eyes on the ball!', Gallwey found that if he asked them to say 'bounce' out loud when the ball bounced and 'hit' out loud when they hit the ball they started to improve markedly. They were automatically keeping their eyes on the ball. Gallwey stopped giving instructions and started to ask questions to help players discover for themselves what worked and what needed to change.

GROW is a simple set of questions that helps you hit the ball in the right direction.

Think

- Who is your mentor?
- And who are you mentoring?

Do

- Use *GROW* to help your team to grow
- Buy a ticket to watch your favourite sport

8e Build trust

If people like you, they'll listen to you, but if they trust you, they'll do business with you.

Zig Ziglar

Terrible News

'I am leaving.'

I was 18 months into my job when the star in my team told me she was joining a direct competitor. I was distraught. This was terrible news for the business and a big blow for me personally. In my first significant leadership role, I had failed to retain the strongest member of the team.

So why did she leave?

She explained that when I had arrived, I shared an exciting vision of a growing business expanding into new areas of work and bringing in new people with new capabilities. This convinced her to stay on. However, over time I had listened to the concerns of the team about previous eras of 'boom and bust', and stuck to our traditional core business and hired no-one. I had failed to implement the vision that had attracted her.

After this I started to invest time in new products and hiring. While it wasn't popular with some of the team, the business grew and became an exciting place to work, full of opportunity. We hired and retained some great people. The big lesson for me was that there can't be a disconnect between what you say you'll do and what you do. The vision must be seen in what you do.

It wasn't that my team saw me hiring again that was important, but that I had started to 'do the vision' again – doing what I said we would do. This engenders trust and commitment.

THE FIVE DYSFUNCTIONS OF A TEAM

Patrick Lencioni, in his book *The Five Dysfunctions of a Team*, identifies five characteristics of dysfunctional teams.

We have seen – and been in – teams that have appeared successful but started to unravel and become dysfunctional. Lencioni identifies five critical areas where the team is the cause of their own downfall, not the competition nor the market conditions. Don't assume everything is okay. Complacency is the enemy.

Lack of trust is the first and most important dysfunction, which leads to the other four.

We have found when working with teams that it can be more constructive to look at the five characteristics positively rather than negatively. So we talk about the positive team characteristic of 'Trust' as opposed to the dysfunctional characteristic of 'Absence of trust'.

Trust starts with every person wanting to achieve the same team goals above personal goals. There is no room for ego. If I believe you want the same thing as I want, and you believe the same of me, we will trust each other. If we don't believe that, trust is damaged.

Trust then allows honest dialogue and *constructive conflict*.

Perhaps counter-intuitively, high performing teams don't find that all is peace and agreement. Rather, they can experience high levels of *conflict*. But the conflict comes not from personal ambition, ego or territory wars – it's always about the best way to achieve the team goal. Constructive conflict allows everyone to have a say and be truly heard. So everyone is able to commit to the team decision, even if they didn't get their way. From this mutual *commitment* everyone is prepared to hold each other to account because the team goal is too important to let people get away with poor performance or missing deadlines.

Accountability means reviewing performance openly, creating the right environment for high performance. This accountability both arises from, and leads to, a *focus on results* – the team's common goal. Any team that is not focusing on its purpose is by definition dysfunctional to the extent that it is focusing on anything else.

Adapted from *The Five Dysfunctions of a Team* by Patrick Lencioni.
See www.tablegroup.com for more tools.

Think

- Who don't you trust in your team? Why?
- Who may not trust you? Why?
- Why might people leave your team?

Do

- Rate your team between 1 and 5 against each factor, starting with 'Trust'. What do you need to work on?
- Do what you need to do to fix the trust issues. Count it a priority
- Add *The Five Dysfunctions of a Team by* Patrick Lencioni to your 'must read' list

Focus 9

Your Life

Everything has been figured out,
except how to live.

Jean-Paul Sartre

Leadership goes beyond the day job.

We have surveyed thousands of business leaders over 25 years, asking them, 'What three changes would you like to make in your life?'

The overwhelming response has been 'A better work/life balance'. Curiously, no-one ever responded with 'Spend more time at the office'.

Sadly, there are too many examples of highly 'successful' people in leadership who leave behind a trail of wreckage in the lives of their teams, their families and their personal lives. The ancient Chinese proverb says 'The fish rots from the head.' If leaders cannot lead themselves and their own lives … beware!

A stocktake on life, and not just work, is time well invested. Lead your own life.

The Life Direction Wheel prompts you to ask questions that you may not have had time to ask yourself recently. There is a *Life Direction Questionnaire* to provoke you to think through these questions at the end of this section. Think about your life as a whole and the choices that you want to make:

Your perspective of your **whole life** – What gives it meaning and what is most important? What are your vision, values and goals?

Your **private life** involves your character, spiritual life and hidden areas. It covers what you want to be, to achieve, to learn and what resources you want to build up and share.

Your **public life** is about family, friendships and your contribution to your community and the wider world.

Your **professional life** comprises your job, your development, your future career and what you want to pass on to others.

THE LIFE DIRECTION WHEEL

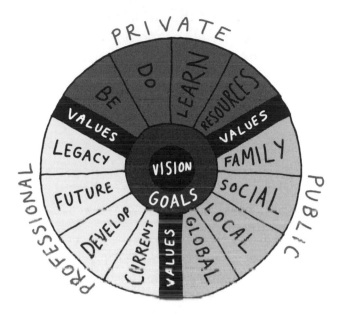

In the following pages we will explore the following principles:

9a Follow your calling

9b Put first things first

9c Keep your integrity

9d Leave a legacy

9e Never give up

9a Follow your calling

Don't ask yourself what the world needs – ask yourself what makes you come alive, and then go do it. Because what the world needs is people who have come alive.

Harold Thurman Whitman

Ebola

'It's really good to be back.'

Will Pooley continued, 'I never meant to leave Sierra Leone. I didn't want to go, so being back feels like I'm back where I should be. I feel like I'm doing a worthwhile job … I'm a nurse and this is where they need nurses.'

In 2014, as the Ebola virus began to devastate Sierra Leone, Will Pooley travelled to work at a hospice in the capital, Freetown. Ebola has fearsome symptoms – high fever and massive internal bleeding. It kills as many as 90% of people it infects. Pooley went straight to the epicentre to help, but became infected himself.

He was flown back to the UK, where he recovered. However, he made the headlines again when he immediately flew back to Sierra Leone to carry on the same gruelling work.

His parents were asked why their son would return and how they cope. Surprisingly, they didn't express worry, but rather pride that Will had found something he loved that made such a difference. 'If he was here he would tell you that he was made to do it.'

Many people feel they are 'made to do' jobs they don't enjoy or value. Here is a man choosing to do a job that could cost him his life.

Are you 'made to do it' because of the demands of your boss or your bank balance … or are you 'made to do it' because that is who you are?

Find out what you are made to do. Follow your calling.

LIFE VISION, VALUES & GOALS

Most of us will admit that, at times, life can be overtaken by the irrelevant or trivial. The *unimportant* can be very noisy and loom large, and the *most important* may be quiet and invisible. If this becomes the norm, the alarm bells should be ringing.

193

Significant events in our lives – new stages of life, new experiences, tragedies, love, loss – can stir us to re-evaluate our lives, even if only momentarily. We shouldn't, however, rely on crises to provoke self-examination.

Socrates said, 'The unexamined life is not worth living.'

What is your purpose?

What is your aim?

Everyone lives for something. For what are you living? We have asked hundreds of leaders what their life purpose is, and surprisingly few can immediately answer.

If you don't know the answer to this question, why are you embarking on any other leadership journey? You may be progressing toward your work vision, but how do you know in terms of your wider life whether you are travelling in the right direction?

Check that you are not like the person who has climbed to the top of the ladder only to discover it was leaning against the wrong building.

Clarity about purpose and direction enables an integrated approach to the whole of life – private, public and professional.

Think

- What do you aspire to in your life? What is your hope for the future?
- What do you daydream about? What preoccupies you?
- Do you have a 'calling'?

Do

- Take one action *today* that will advance your hope for the future. Do the same tomorrow. And the day after
- Re-evaluate your giving to your chosen charities

9b Put first things first

You always have time for the things you put first.

Anon

Rain or Snow

I looked across the field and there was dad clapping.

I didn't think it was that unusual that my dad watched every sporting match or race that I was in. I thought that was just what dads do.

He had a very demanding job on the board of the *Financial Times*, yet he would arrange his work to fit in with me and my sporting schedule. I wasn't the best in the team, but I know I did much better than I would have done because Dad was there. For ten years, rain or snow, regardless of train trouble or bad traffic, he was there.

Once I started working and couldn't even get away at 6pm, I started to wonder how he managed to do it. I found myself rushing around and crises seemed to pop up just as I wanted to leave. However, my children are now in teams, and guess what? I'm not going to miss their games.

The fact that I was such a priority for my dad has given me confidence. His investment has truly paid dividends in my life. I remember the journeys home, and I can picture him on the touchline even now.

I want the same for my children, so I've made that a priority. It may not seem important to them now, but in ten years it will bear fruit.

And maybe in 20 years' time, my kids will watch all their kids' matches.

What are you prioritising today that will bear fruit in five or ten years' time?

THE BUCKET RACE

We have used the bucket race to great effect with many leadership groups.

The group is divided into small teams. Each team is given a large bucket and some materials – a pile of fine sand, a load of pebbles, three bricks and a quantity of water. All the materials can fit into the bucket perfectly without going above the rim.

The winning team is the team that can fill the empty bucket with all the materials without going over the rim and race 25m to a finishing line. (The race is not essential, but fun. Make sure it is outside, as it can get messy!) If the materials go above the rim of the bucket, the team is disqualified.

Sounds simple.

We have seen teams make all sorts of mistakes as they pile in the materials quickly in an effort to get to the finish line first. Often teams find that they have to start over again as the contents spill out over the rim. It looks very messy as they scoop out wet, pebbly sand.

There is only one way to succeed – put the bricks in first. Then the pebbles, carefully filling the gaps between the bricks. Next comes the fine sand, which takes up the rest of the space. After some careful banging of the bucket on the ground to sift the sand right down to the bottom of the bucket, the water can then be poured in. Finally, it's the 25m dash!

The message is simple. Put the big stuff in first!

Putting it in second just doesn't work.

It's the same in life. If we don't put the big stuff in first – the most important things – the space is taken up with something of secondary importance.

Think

- What 'big stuff' in your life is getting squeezed out?
- What secondary things are dominating your time?

Do

- Put a brick on your desk for the next month to help remind you to put first things first

9c Keep your integrity

It takes 20 years to build a reputation and five minutes to ruin it. Think about that and you'll do things differently.
Warren Buffett

A Seat on the Bus

Rosa McCauley had dignity and self-esteem.

She decided at school that she would not '[set her] sights lower than anybody, just because [she] was black. We were taught to believe that we could do whatever we wanted in life.' However, in the 1930s and 1940s, African Americans in the USA lived in a world of separate drinking fountains, separate restrooms and separate elevators. Rosa avoided using these facilities and took the stairs rather than live 'divided'.

In 1943, Rosa McCauley Parks was refused entrance to the 'whites only' front entrance of a packed bus by the driver, James F. Blake. She refused ever again to board a bus he was driving.

In 1955 the National Association for the Advancement of Colored People (NAACP) needed someone to make a stand against the City of Montgomery, Alabama, for its, by now, illegal policy of segregation on public transport. They chose Rosa.

So on 1 December she once again boarded a bus driven by James F Blake, but this time she refused his demand to give up her seat to a white man. 'I was not tired physically', she later reported, 'I was tired of giving in'. Blake called the police and she was arrested.

Rosa, who had been teased by her friends for being a 'goody-goody', became a convicted criminal because of her convictions about equality. Once released, she vowed never again to ride a segregated bus. The black community rallied around her stand and boycotted the Montgomery public buses for an incredible 381 days.

Rosa lost her job and suffered frequent death threats but became the mother of the civil rights movement. In 1956, the US Supreme Court ruled that it was unconstitutional to segregate riders on city buses. In 1964, the Civil Rights Act guaranteed African Americans the right to vote and outlawed segregation in all public accommodations.

The word integrity comes from the Latin *integer* meaning 'whole'. Keeping your integrity means being undivided and acting according to the values, beliefs and principles you hold. Integrity cannot be kept in just one compartment of your life. For Rosa Parks, it had to permeate the whole of her life. A life of integrity is whole and undivided.

Having integrity is an essential attribute to success in life and in business. This means making decisions that are not simply expedient, but have long-term value.

THE TRUSTED ADVISER

David Maister, author of *The Trusted Advisor* and former Harvard Business School professor and world-renowned consultant, developed the Trusted Advisor model. He concluded that his clients came to him first and foremost because they trusted him, rather than because of his technical expertise. There are legions of technical experts, but people choose to work with the ones they trust.

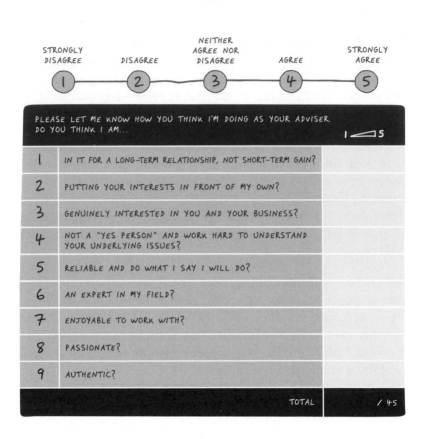

	STRONGLY DISAGREE	DISAGREE	NEITHER AGREE NOR DISAGREE	AGREE	STRONGLY AGREE
	1	2	3	4	5

PLEASE LET ME KNOW HOW YOU THINK I'M DOING AS YOUR ADVISER. DO YOU THINK I AM... 1 ◁ 5

1	IN IT FOR A LONG-TERM RELATIONSHIP, NOT SHORT-TERM GAIN?	
2	PUTTING YOUR INTERESTS IN FRONT OF MY OWN?	
3	GENUINELY INTERESTED IN YOU AND YOUR BUSINESS?	
4	NOT A "YES PERSON" AND WORK HARD TO UNDERSTAND YOUR UNDERLYING ISSUES?	
5	RELIABLE AND DO WHAT I SAY I WILL DO?	
6	AN EXPERT IN MY FIELD?	
7	ENJOYABLE TO WORK WITH?	
8	PASSIONATE?	
9	AUTHENTIC?	
	TOTAL	/ 45

Although we often don't realise it, people can spot mixed motives in our behaviour. We may only call them when we want something. Yet clients and stakeholders prefer regular contact with their advisers outside of the confines of specific projects. Trusted advisers invest time in counselling and actively look out for the best interests of their clients and their people.

Ultimately, trusted advisers will put their clients' interests ahead of their own. On several occasions, I have turned down work because I didn't think it was in the client's interests – or even done it for free because I thought it was essential. I wasn't thinking of this as a 'sales technique', but it has positioned me as a trusted adviser.

Integrity is fundamental to building trusted relationships.

Think

- What is your reputation?
- Where is your own integrity tested most?
- How would you score yourself on the Trusted Advisor survey?

Do

- Make one decision or take one action that will help you to protect or enhance your personal integrity

9d Leave a legacy

The ultimate measure of a man is not where he stands in times of comfort, but where he stands at times of challenge and controversy.

Martin Luther King Jr

Buried in the Rubble

The bomb exploded.

It was 8 November 1987. The IRA had detonated a bomb in Enniskillen, Northern Ireland, killing 11 people and injuring 64. Gordon Wilson and his daughter, Marie, were buried in rubble. Unable to move, he held her hand and comforted her as she lay dying.

Her last words were, 'Daddy, I love you very much.'

In an interview with the BBC, Wilson said, 'I bear no ill will. I bear no grudge. Dirty sort of talk is not going to bring her back to life. She was a great wee lassie. She loved her profession. She was a pet. She's dead. She's in heaven and we shall meet again. I will pray for these men tonight and every night.'

As historian Jonathan Bardon recounts, 'No words in more than 25 years of violence in Northern Ireland had such a powerful, emotional impact.'

Subsequently, the IRA issued a statement offering 'sincerest condolences and apologies' for his daughter's death. In 1989 Wilson helped launch a community outreach programme entitled the Spirit of Enniskillen Trust, which helped young people in Northern Ireland participate in international programmes and gave bursaries to promote reconciliation in Northern Ireland.

The BBC later described the bombing as a turning point in the troubles. Pivotal to the change in attitude toward this sort of attack was Wilson's reaction to the death of his daughter.

Leave the legacy you want.

What do you want to leave for others?

RATE YOUR LIFE

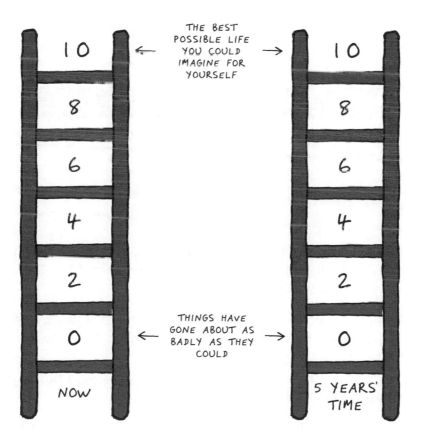

Peter Flade, formerly of Gallup, uses a challenging group exercise that can help you consider the legacy you might leave now. He gets everyone to stand up and to imagine a ladder with ten rungs. They are to rate their life and wellbeing now from zero to ten. Zero is where things have gone about as badly as they could and ten is the best possible life you could imagine for yourself.

He then asks people to sit down if they scored four or below; then six or below, etc. Less than 5% will remain standing at nine and only 1% at ten.

Then he asks you to score where you think your life will be in five years. Gallup's research in over 160 countries shows people score their anticipated future lives as follows:

SCORE	CATEGORY	% OF GLOBAL POPULATION
0–4	SUFFERING	13%
5–6	STRUGGLING	60–64%
7–10	THRIVING	23–27%

If, like half the population in the USA and UK, you are struggling today and still think you will be in five years' time, it's unlikely that you will leave the legacy you want.

Gallup's research over many years shows that five things increase happiness and fulfilment and will help you leave the legacy you want:

1. *Purpose.* Do you enjoy what you do every day? Did you do or learn something interesting yesterday?

2. *Social.* Spending about six hours a day with people you love and who love you back. Work can play a key role here

because we spend so much time at work, and stress at work can negatively impact home life.

3. *Financial.* Money will help you leave a financial legacy, but our happiness only increases as we earn enough money to meet our relatively simple needs. After annual household income reaches the national average, our happiness stays the same.

4. *Physical.* Having the energy to do most of what you want to do. Even those with long-term illnesses can be happy so long as they have the energy and ability to do what they enjoy.

5. *Community.* Giving back to others, for instance by giving blood, coaching a team, helping in your neighbourhood, supporting a cause and being part of a faith community.

Think

- Who left you a legacy?
- Rate your life now.
- What score do you want?

Do

- Plan to do something great three months from today. Put it in your calendar
- Write or update your will
- Write your 'Will of Intangibles' – the intangible benefits that you want to pass on to specific people

9e Never give up

If at first you don't succeed, skydiving is not for you.
Steven Wright

10,000 Ways That Won't Work

'Your Tommy is too stupid to learn. We cannot have him at our school.'

Tommy, aged four, gave the note to his mother. He'd just been sent home from school. Young Tommy was something of a dreamer. If there had been a school psychologist, he would probably have been diagnosed with attention deficit disorder.

If you are a parent, with normal aspirations for your child, this is a letter that would either make you fume or cry, or both. This would not be the last setback young Tommy would face – there would be 10,000 more.

Tommy – or Thomas Edison, as he became better known – knew about setbacks. He famously failed in his quest to produce an electric light bulb 10,000 times before he finally succeeded. Or as he put it: 'I have not failed. I've just found 10,000 ways that won't work.'

He knew how to dream, but also how not to give up in the face of disappointment. He knew what it was to be resilient and also to keep learning. Edison went on to have over 2,000 patents to his name. His many inventions have transformed our modern world.

When something doesn't work out, it's important to face the reality but not lose sight of the fact that there are other ways forward. Leaders are dealers in *truth*, but they are also dealers in *hope*.

Psychologist Martin Seligman, in his book *Learned Optimism*, shows that the pessimist, when facing a difficulty, is likely to believe that bad events will last a long time. The optimist, in the same circumstances, believes that defeat is just a temporary setback.

THE LEARNING CYCLE

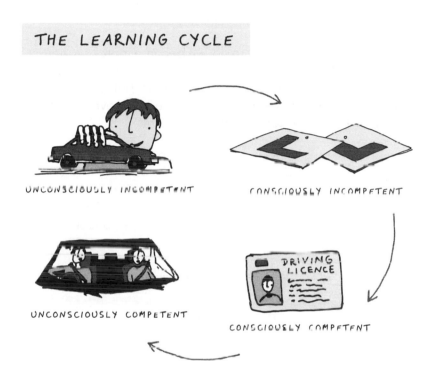

UNCONSCIOUSLY INCOMPETENT

CONSCIOUSLY INCOMPETENT

UNCONSCIOUSLY COMPETENT

CONSCIOUSLY COMPETENT

All of us go through a learning cycle, just as Thomas Edison did.

We begin not knowing what we don't know – blissful ignorance, or the state of being 'unconsciously incompetent'. As we start the learning process, the first realisation is just how much we don't know, and how much we will need to learn.

Think of learning to drive. What appeared to be little more than pressing a pedal and turning a wheel suddenly has us lurching and bouncing kangaroo-like along public roads. What seemed simple suddenly feels daunting.

How will we *ever* master this skill? We can get despondent and want to give up, but we can't go back to our state of blissful ignorance. We have progressed to 'conscious incompetence'. Now we know – in part – the scale of the project.

As we start to work out what to do, we become more competent. If we practise – repeating 'mirror, signal, manoeuvre' quietly under our breath – we realise we can do it. But it takes great concentration and huge mental, and perhaps even physical, energy. We are now 'consciously competent'.

Then, imperceptibly, as we continue to practise and learn, the newly learned skills become easier and easier until it becomes second nature to us. We end up driving along roads on auto-pilot, hardly aware of the road behind us. It takes little energy. We have reached the goal; we have become 'unconsciously competent'.

'Be Resilient' and 'Keep Learning' should be two friends who constantly travel with you on the journey.

Think

- How resilient are you?
- What good things have you stopped halfway through? Why did you stop?
- Are you currently considering giving up on something? Why?

Do

- Invest in your learning
- Keep on keeping on with the things which are most important
- Complete the *Life Direction Questionnaire*

LIFE DIRECTION QUESTIONNAIRE

WHOLE LIFE

VISION

1. WHAT IS YOUR PRIMARY PURPOSE IN LIFE? [PERSONAL MEANING]

VALUES

2. WHAT ARE YOUR THREE MOST IMPORTANT PERSONAL VALUES OR GOLDEN RULES? [LIFE PRINCIPLES]

GOALS

3. WHAT ARE YOUR TOP THREE GOALS IN LIFE? [ACHIEVEMENTS BY "LIFE'S END"]

PRIVATE LIFE (YOU)

BE

4. HOW DO YOU WANT TO DEVELOP IN YOUR CHARACTER, INNER BEING OR SPIRITUAL LIFE? [INDIVIDUAL FULFILMENT, DEVELOPMENT OF POTENTIAL, BELIEFS]

DO

5. WHAT DO YOU WANT TO DO OR ACHIEVE IN YOUR PRIVATE LIFE? [INDIVIDUAL ACHIEVEMENTS, CULTURE/SPORT/ RECREATION, PLANS FOR RETIREMENT]

LEARN

6. WHAT DO YOU WANT TO LEARN OR DEVELOP SKILLS IN? [EDUCATION, HOBBIES, LANGUAGES, PRACTICAL SKILLS]

RESOURCES

7. WHAT ARE YOUR PLANS FOR YOUR FINANCES AND OTHER PRACTICAL RESOURCES? [FINANCIAL GOALS, PROPERTY/POSSESSIONS, WILL/LEGACY]

PUBLIC LIFE (YOU & OTHERS)

FAMILY 8. WHAT ARE YOUR ASPIRATIONS FOR YOUR CLOSEST RELATIONSHIPS/FAMILY LIFE? [PARTNER, CLOSE FRIENDS, NUCLEAR AND EXTENDED FAMILY]

SOCIAL 9. WHAT WIDER RELATIONSHIPS AND ACTIVITIES DO YOU WANT TO PURSUE AND ENJOY? [FRIENDSHIPS, SPORTS/HOBBY CLUBS, CULTURAL ACTIVITIES]

LOCAL 10. WHAT DO YOU WANT TO DO IN YOUR LOCAL COMMUNITY? [NEIGHBOURHOOD/VOLUNTARY ACTIVITY, FAITH GROUP]

GLOBAL 11. WHAT DO YOU WANT TO DO IN THE WIDER WORLD? [CHARITY ACTIVITIES, CAUSES, POLITICS]

PROFESSIONAL LIFE (YOU & WORK)

CURRENT 12. WHAT DO YOU WANT TO DELIVER IN YOUR CURRENT ROLE? [ACHIEVEMENTS]

DEVELOP 13. HOW DO YOU WANT TO DEVELOP PROFESSIONALLY? [FUTURE CAPABILITIES]

FUTURE 14. HOW DO YOU WANT YOUR CAREER TO PROGRESS? [FUTURE OPPORTUNITIES AND ROLES]

LEGACY 15. HOW DO YOU WANT TO BE REMEMBERED IN YOUR WORK LIFE? [REPUTATION, INFLUENCE, WHAT YOU WANT TO PASS ON TO OTHERS]

LEAD
Self-assessment

Through *LEAD* you have covered the three key priorities of leaders:

1. Map

2. Navigate

3. Grow

Nine areas of focus have been covered through the *Dashboard*.

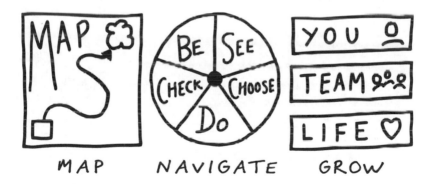

In each of these areas we have identified key principles that will enable you to lead successfully. Use the following *LEAD* self-assessment to assess yourself against these principles.

LEAD

SELF ASSESSMENT

MAP   NAVIGATE   GROW

SCORE YOURSELF AGAINST EACH PRINCIPLE BELOW

LOW 1   2   3   4   5 HIGH

DEVELOP YOUR STRATEGY ON A PAGE:					
UNDERSTAND YOUR CHANGING CONTEXT					
KEEP PLOTTING YOUR JOURNEY					

MAP   /10

UNDERSTAND THE WHY					
THINK OUTSIDE-IN					
MAKE THE CONNECTIONS					
LOOK INSIDE THE BOX					
TAKE THE LONG VIEW					

SEE THE BIG PICTURE /25

START WITH THE END IN MIND					
PRIORITISE YOUR PRIORITIES					
CHOOSE YOUR GOLDEN RULES					
SET THE RIGHT GOALS					
COMMUNICATE THE COURSE					

CHOOSE THE RIGHT DIRECTION /25

BE TRANSFORMATIVE					
BE CREATIVE					
BE PROACTIVE					
BE PRODUCTIVE					
BE REACTIVE? (1=TOO REACTIVE)					

DO THE RIGHT THINGS /25

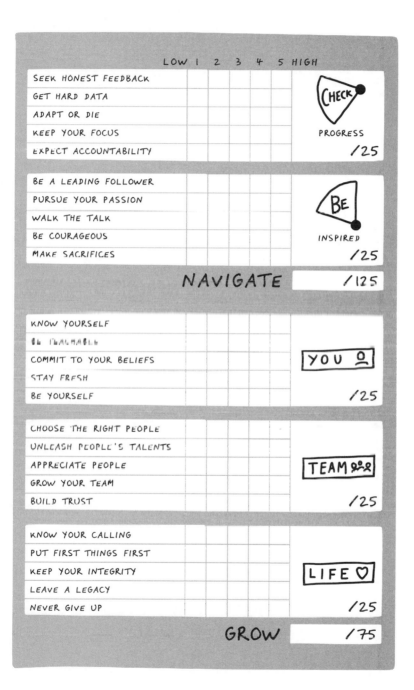

	LOW 1	2	3	4	5 HIGH	
SEEK HONEST FEEDBACK						
GET HARD DATA						CHECK
ADAPT OR DIE						
KEEP YOUR FOCUS						PROGRESS
EXPECT ACCOUNTABILITY						/25

BE A LEADING FOLLOWER						
PURSUE YOUR PASSION						BE
WALK THE TALK						
BE COURAGEOUS						INSPIRED
MAKE SACRIFICES						/25

NAVIGATE /125

KNOW YOURSELF						
BE TEACHABLE						
COMMIT TO YOUR BELIEFS						YOU
STAY FRESH						
BE YOURSELF						/25

CHOOSE THE RIGHT PEOPLE						
UNLEASH PEOPLE'S TALENTS						
APPRECIATE PEOPLE						TEAM
GROW YOUR TEAM						
BUILD TRUST						/25

KNOW YOUR CALLING						
PUT FIRST THINGS FIRST						
KEEP YOUR INTEGRITY						LIFE
LEAVE A LEGACY						
NEVER GIVE UP						/25

GROW /75

What Next?

Having completed the *LEAD* self-assessment, you should have a better view of what you need and want to do next.

Walt Disney's advice in such circumstances could be useful: 'The way to get started is to quit talking and begin doing.'

We hope that you are clearer about where you are headed and more confident that you will get there.

We know for sure that it won't be simple because ... life is not a straight line! But we hope that it will be immensely rewarding and great fun.

May you lead and succeed well in work and life ... and may others benefit.

Thanks

Life is just like an old-time train journey . . . delays, side-tracks, smoke, dust, cinders and jolts, interspersed only by beautiful vistas and thrilling bursts of speed. The trick is to thank the Lord for letting you have the ride.

Jenkin Lloyd Jones

Additionally, we have a few other people to thank.

The illustrations are the work of Bryan Mathers. What a talented man and the perfect collaborator – clear about our purpose, challenging and conscientious. A superb visual thinker.

Annie Knight, Chloe Satchell-Cobbett and Tessa Allen at Wiley have been great partners and the catalyst to getting this book published.

LEAD is a crystallisation of many of the things that we have experienced and learnt over years of working with friends, colleagues and business leaders, for which we say a very big thank you. We are particularly grateful to each one who has reviewed *LEAD* and given us feedback, especially Jackie Greenway.

We are very grateful to Colin Price, Mercuri Urval, Belbin, John Kotter and Harvard Business Publishing, who kindly gave us permission to use their material.

Finally, we want to express our great gratitude to our respective families for their great love and support and surprising interest in what we do.

About the Authors

John D H Greenway loves helping people find their purpose, clarify their priorities and fulfil their potential. He has 30 years' experience working with business leaders to build winning teams. He distilled his insights into his first book, *Leaders' Map: helping doers think and thinkers do.*

After graduating from Nottingham and Durham Universities, he has led business divisions, directed global accounts, sat on boards, worked with aid organisations and coached sports teams. He and his wife live in central London and are involved in the leadership of a thriving, multi-cultural church. They have three adult children and an ever-expanding clan.

Andy Blacknell's passion is helping leaders and organisations to engage their people. With a history degree from the University of Oxford, he started work as an economist co-authoring books on the European Union and management development. He then worked for a major UK retailer, Woolworths and saw first-hand how difficult it is to lead change.

As a partner at Willis Towers Watson, he has worked in the USA and UK on some of the world's largest mergers and measured the engagement of millions of employees. He runs his own consulting business, Blacknell Ventures.

He and his wife Alex have four children.

Andy Coombe is a leadership facilitator. He enables people to have the conversations they need to have to bring vitality and success to work and life. He has a master's degree in organisational change from the University of Bristol. Before that he studied philosophy and theology at the University of Southampton. He has extensive operational and change advisory experience in the UK health sector, working with boards as both a director of an acute hospital trust and leading a change consultancy.

Andy now leads Kairos Consultancy, which focuses on leadership and organisational development. He is also engaged in executive coaching, mediation and large event facilitation. Andy works with his wife, Helen, who leads the Kairos work in international development. They have two daughters.

In whatever time is left Andy runs marathons.

Index

INDEX